The Horizon Unveiled

Published by
FGD Tanzania Limited
P. O. Box 40331
Dar es Salaam
Tanzania
Email: booksbyfgd@gmail.com

@ Fellowes Mwaisela, 2018

Second Edition

ISBN 978 9987 483 19 8

Contents

To my uncle Ulimbakisya Ikumboka
for sending me to school

To my wife Stella, my sons Lugano and Elisha
for their love.

"... an individual who feels comfortable only in his or her clan is still being held back from full realization of his or her potentialities as a human being...And finally, an individual whose horizons are limited to the borders of his or her own country or society is yet sensitized to the international implications of social existence."

-Mazrui, *Swahili States and Society*

PROLOGUE

When I was about six years old, I looked at the horizon and simply considered it as a line that separated the mountains in the distance from the blue sky. To me, it was the edge of the earth. It was a security cordon against falling into the bottomless abyss. Thus, I believed that there was no life beyond the line.

The other image that came into my mind when I looked at the horizon, was that of a big bowl and a lid made of glass. I felt as if our village, Ilinga, was inside a big bowl and the sky was the lid that covered the bowl. The horizon therefore was where the bowl's and the lid's edges touched.

I felt like I was inside the bowl and I could not go beyond the point where it met with the lid. Because the lid was made of glass I could see beyond our village. Ilalabwe, the village of my maternal grandmother, seemed to lie by the horizon.

Ilalabwe was situated at the foot of Nyika Mountains. It therefore, seemed to me that if one stood on top of Nyika Mountains, he or she could touch the 'lid' that covered the big 'bowl'. What I innocently believed, therefore, was that one standing on top of the Mountains could touch the sky.

I spent most of my time then playing around home. Sometimes I looked at the horizon in the direction of Ilalabwe, where my mother was born. Mount Rungwe, on the other direction, was more than a physical feature. It stood like a king's guard, at the gate of the royal garden, protecting the land. Most of the morning the 'guard' took advantage of the cloud camouflage.

At that time I thought the horizon was where the earth and heaven met. I was not the only one troubled by the orientation of the universe. One day I overheard a conversation from a group of people at a church near our home. Though he was not present on that day I knew, however, that my paternal grandfather planted what they called "Last Church" in the village. The congregants were separate from the local Moravian church where my father ministered.

A man asked: *"Kali ku Amerika kokugu bagwitu."*

Another man replied: "America is where the sun sets, but beyond."

For me, at the age of six, I could not imagine that there were people living beyond the horizon. This, I believed, was the very place where the sun set. Moreover, I didn't think that there could be other people speaking a different language. Of course, I was aware of a relatively small community of Waswahili in Tukuyu, the major business town in our district. They spoke Kiswahili. But that seemed to be an exceptional case. My general thinking was that everybody wherever he or she was spoke Kinyakyusa. This myth remained with me until when I travelled from our village to my grandmother's village then to Mbeya town.

Over time, fate shattered that myth and though it was scary, it made me part of a larger experience. I have had many opportunities to travel to many places inside and outside Tanzania. I was 41 the first time I travelled out of the country. The year was 1997. A lady at the check in desk said: "Mr. Fellowes Mwaisela, here is your boarding pass. Have a safe journey." I smiled broadly, curious about the borders beyond my country.

CHAPTER 1

IN THE BOWL OF NAIVETY

I was born to farming parents in a hardly known small village of Ilinga just on the outskirts of Tukuyu town. My father was of a dark complexion, had a stern voice, penetrating eyes and was five feet and some inches tall. He had a moustache, which together with the penetrating eyes gave him the look of a cop. His face got a bit wrinkled when he smoked his filterless 10 Cents brand cigarette as he sat on his chair in the evening. He would have spent most of the day doing church work.

Unlike most other male adults in the village, he never took *pombe*. His favourite drink was tea with milk. He would take several cups of tea a day. His last cup would be at around 10 pm. Then he would turn off his radio and go to bed. He would wake up at 5 am and take his first cup of tea before leaving his bed.

I do not remember hearing him talk about when he and my mother got married. My guess is that it could have been in 1956 because my brother, Daniel, was born in 1957. Two years later, April 24, 1959, I was born. My mother, Malita, came from Ilalabwe, a village about fifteen kilometres away from ours.

My father and mother were primarily involved in farming. They cultivated coffee, banana, maize and beans. Coffee was grown as a cash crop while banana, maize and beans were used as food crops. Apart from farming activities my father was a trader, he bought fish from Lake Nyasa or Lake Rukwa and sold them at the market in Tukuyu.

On Sundays, he would lead a service at the village church. The church service started at around 10 am and ended at around 12 noon. But he would not return home until around 6pm in the evening. After the service he would visit the sick and the elderly. He normally carried aspirin tablets with him. He himself was not at the best of his health, but that did not hinder him from making the visits.

At home he was a family "medical doctor" for us all and a "veterinary doctor" for his cows. He applied medicinal plants. I especially recall one night when I had a serious stomach ache. It was about midnight. I could not take the pains any more. I woke him up. He fetched a small bit of a dried root from his skin bag that he kept in his room. He asked me to chew and swallow the saliva. I chewed the bit. It was so bitter and sour that I wanted to spit it. "Now, you'll chew it, *asee!*" It was clear from the tone of his voice that he did not mean any non-sense. I chewed and swallowed. In a moment I didn't feel pain anymore.

The following morning I asked him:

"What was that medicine that you gave me?"

"Pupwe," he replied in his heavy voice.

Since then, I have never been relieved from stomach ache by other medicine in such a short moment. Whenever our cows got sick, he mainly used *iloboka*, although on several other occasions he used other medicinal plants.

But all in all his major occupation was banana and coffee farming. The banana and coffee *shamba* formed a U shape around our house. The only remaining portion was the front side, which was covered with grass.

And my friends and I used it as a play ground. It was also from this place that I pondered the horizon and beyond. And sometimes we would see an aircraft in the sky "*akaroketi*, a rocket," we would shout.

Also standing at the playground I was fascinated by the way the main path from town branched into two when it reached the compound of our house. The two branches went beyond our village, one to the left and the other to the right. I would recall the day my mother and I went to Ilalabwe, we took the left path and crossed several streams: Lina, Sasa, Sabilo and several others, until it reached my grandmother's village. The right path went down a hill across a stream then uphill until it reached on top of the hill where there was my father's church. Our home located where the two paths joined towards town and parted toward the interior of the village was at a unique position. One could not miss it. This also made it natural for us to see those coming in and going out of the village.

On the day when farmers received payment after selling coffee to a cooperative society, many people would stream into town. Joy that accompanied payday clear on their faces. They looked youthful and excited. They were smart, probably in clothes from the bottom of their boxes. They greeted everyone they met on the way with a broad smile. The office building of the Cooperative Society towered high at the centre of Tukuyu town and it posed with confidence. In those days, I never heard my father complaining about delayed payment from sales of their coffee.

With the money he earned from coffee my father was able to build a second house. In those days, a homestead consisted of two buildings, the main house, *itikalifu*, and the kitchen, detached from the former. He hired a man called Bene to make bricks from clay. Bene dug a ditch not far from the house we lived in and from there he obtained the clay for the bricks. The house is still there today.

Bene, the bricks maker, was not a member of our ethnic group. In those days, it was common for members of his tribe to look for jobs in our area. It was said that they came from the mountains. With them they brought wooden handcrafts and pots for sale. They were also known to be good at lumber jacking.

He was a nice joyful guy. He looked

younger than my father. He had beard on his chin that made him look even friendlier. With his slender body he looked relaxed all the time. I never saw him angry. I felt comfortable in his presence. In the evening, he would tell us stories by the fire side. I became attached to him and felt that his presence made our family complete. He himself would be laughing while telling the stories. He laughed in his own style. When he laughed his entire body shook. His laughing style would make you laugh even before he had finished telling the story.

From our house compound I would also watch many women of all ages carrying baskets full of ripe bananas on their heads. They would sell the bananas at the market or on the sides of the main road. They greeted us whenever they passed by our house.

For one to go to town from our village, one had to pass through a small forest, *pabusisya*. It was a cool and potentially frightening place. There were many scary stories surrounding the forest. There were those who claimed to have seen a very tall creature in the shape of a man and four times taller the height of a grown up person. They claimed that such a creature always put on a long white gown. Not many were brave enough to cross this forest during the night without the company of people they knew. So the timings of going in and out of the village to the shops in town seemed to be controlled by the *pabusisya*. As one walked from our village towards the district headquarters (*Bomani*) he would first see the shop that belonged to an African trader, the second belonged to an Arab, the third to a Somali and the rest along the way to the *Boma*, belonged to Indians.

I remember my father taking me to one of the Indian shops. He wanted to know whether the piece of cloth he had given one of the tailors to make a shirt for my school uniform was ready. The shop had a big veranda with about four tailors. They were busy operating the sewing machines. Their machines rattled in unison *ta , ta,ta,ta…*

My father to the tailor: Good morning.
The tailor to my father: Good morning.
My father to the tailor: Is the shirt ready?
The tailor to my father: Not yet.
My father to the tailor: Mmmh! what?
The tailor to my father: You know what, your cloth is a very special one. It needs a

special thread. So I have sent someone to Mbeya. There he will be able to find the right one. There is no shop here where you can find the thread.

My father to the tailor: So, when should I come to fetch it?

The tailor to my father: Very soon it will be ready. Just walk around and come after two hours.

The Indian shop buildings were designed in such a way that over the veranda of each shop there was a canopy to protect the tailors from rain or the afternoon sun. Around the canopy were fixed electric bulbs of different colours. The common colours were green, yellow, blue and red. When dusk came they were put on and they blossomed like roses!

The situation looked even rosier at the two Indian temples where there were more coloured bulbs fixed around the lintel. In the evenings, the red, green yellow and blue bulbs glowed light as the believers flocked in. With the coloured bulbs glowing, Tukuyu down town seemed to lure everyone to visit the place and stay there.

After sunset, was normally very dark in my village. And it was forbidden to talk about certain things. Above all, in the forbidden list was a legendary snake called *njoka*. It was rumoured that the snake had many heads. The heads were positioned in Lake Nyasa, at certain points in river Kiwira and on Mount Rungwe. It was further rumoured that if you succeeded in getting a piece of its skin you would be free from all sorts of dangers. Even in serious accidents you would come out without a scratch. It was said that getting a piece of *njoka* skin was possible with the help of medicine men.

It was also rumoured that people of the land had their own snake. It was said that the snake maintained the fertility of the land. Unknowingly, one man killed it. When the elders heard this, they ordered him to buy a white cloth so that he would tie the two pieces of the snake together. Then they told him to walk away from the scene without looking back. It was believed that after the ritual the snake became alive again.

I did not know whether my father believed the story of snake. May be, his Christian faith or status, as a church elder, prevented him from believing or showing that he believed. He led a congregation of about one hundred and fifty Christians. The church where my father preached was built on top of one of the several ridges in the area. From our home to the church, we had to cross two streams. Crossing of the second stream was followed by an immediate climb through a narrow slippery path.

Just like the school, the church used a wheel rim for a bell. The wheel rim was tied to a rope and hung from a tree branch. So, the deacon would hit it with an iron bar, about six inches in length, to produce a sound that reminded people that the service was about to start.

Going to the church always excited me. I enjoyed touching the cold stream water and listening to Bible stories.

My father went to church every Sunday, unless he was sick or if he had to attend village meetings. The meetings were normally held on Sunday mornings. The agenda of the meetings ranged from petty misunderstandings between wife and husband to land disputes.

There were respected elders who mediated the conflicting parties or simply passed a ruling. It seems the elders were able to resolve the conflicts successfully. I do not remember any incidence of violence that was associated with an unresolved conflict.

Despite minor disputes, the situation in the village was generally calm.

Then one day my sister saw a mole making a hole into our house. She told our father about it. He found a stick and hit it, killing it instantly and burnt the carcass. After a few days he started feeling terrible pains on his right hand. It was so painful that he stopped working his farm. However, this did not hinder my father from undertaking other responsibilities. Every morning he would ride his Gazelle brand bicycle to the central market to sell fish. He also continued with his duties at the church, especially that of teaching the youth preparing themselves for confirmation.

The mole incident was far from the strangest village occurrence. A man called Mwakyelusya went around the villages arresting people suspected to be witches. He had a team of women who would sing while he tied the 'culprits'. A piece of a bamboo pole would be tightened across the culprit's legs until he revealed all his or her fetishes. The fetishes were then collected and burnt. He went from one place to another claiming to cleanse the land of witchcraft.

Then, there was a man named Nnsyuka.
This man, so it was said, led a very rough
life. When he died, according to rumours,
he tested the hell fire. But while there in
the world of the dead somehow he was
pardoned and given one more chance to
live on earth so that he could provide his
testimony and repent.

One day, I was attending a church service
in Tukuyu town and this man happened to
be there. "That is Nnsyuka" a man next
to me whispered. Nnsyuka was probably
in his late forties. He was in a brown shirt
and white trousers. Marks of an apparently
severe burn were still visible on his hands.
The testimony of Nnsyuka reinforced in me
what the Sunday school teacher taught us
about life after death and the eternal fire.

Then there was the legendary thief
called Mwanhiji. It was said that the most
notorious part of his "profession" was that
he could not die in the way other people
would die. His story was one of those
stories that grandparents narrated at night
when children were around the fire. He was
considered to be the most notorious among
cattle rustlers in the area. He would secretly
go to house from which he intends to steal.

In those days people shared the same house with their cattle. He would then make a hole in the wall. Then he would push in a banana tree trunk. He smeared the front part of the trunk with black ash to make it look like a man's head. He did this to check if the owners were already asleep. He assumed that if the owner was awake he would react by hitting the 'head'. This would signify danger and he would run away. But the trick did not always work to his favour. On several occasions he was caught and beaten severely. But to the disappointment of his catchers, the next day they would hear that Mwanhiji was alive and had managed to steal cattle in another village.

The other types of "thieves" were tax collectors. They came in the village and arrested men who had not paid poll tax. Unlike Mwanhiji, they came in broad day light but when people least expected them, ambush men of tax eligible age. However, ambushes by tax collectors never worked on one person- Lubilo. This man was extremely good at running. None of the tax collectors matched his running ability.

Most admirable to me, however, among all the legends, was the driver Salama

Salimini (SS). He used to roll his long sleeve shirt above his elbow. That way his built up biceps muscles became visible. He had a long beard and a fixed smile. His eyes were large, inviting yet concentrating. The eyes added to his charming nature. But his charming did not dilute his potentiality to be serious when it was necessary. He hardly combed his hair properly but this did not make people lose faith in him as far as safe driving was concerned. He was a respected driver. It was said that he had never had an accident. He was especially known for making dramatic escape. He saved a friend from highway robbers.

One day, he drove a Land Rover to an undisclosed place. On the way, according to the story he cut two branches and hid them by the road side. Then, he managed to reach a place where his friend was hiding. His friend boarded the car and both sped away. SS stopped the car where he had hid the two branches. He quickly tied the branches below the rear door. The branches were tied in such a way that they touched the road, which had no tarmac. As the car sped towards a safe house, it left behind a huge cloud of dust. The dust caused poor visibility for the car giving a chase from behind. In that way, SS left the robbers at a distance, taking his friend to a safe house.

This story was retold several times by different people in town. Some villagers who went into town heard it and brought it to the village. Whenever, I saw Salama Salimini, the driver, some questions remained with me unanswered. Was he rewarded for the mission, how much was the reward worth?

Back in the village, Mwanndimi was a celebrity in his own right when it came to tilling the land. His *shamba* was always clean. He would always be the first to clear his farm during the maize and beans planting season. It was widely rumoured that he drew his strength and stamina from smoking. He grew some tobacco plants close to the cowshed in his compound. So, he would pick leaves from the plants, dry them and make for himself the smoking stuff. He normally did this by putting the dry leaves on his left palm, which he crushed with his right hand thumb, ending up with small particles. He would then carefully balance the particles with the index and middle fingers on an old piece of paper torn out of paper bag. Once the material was properly in place, he would smear the hanging end of the paper with his saliva. In the end, he would be smoking his 'cigarette'.

His wife would always be ready to bring him a burning piece of firewood, a *kisinga*. The combination of smoke from the *kisinga* and the one released from his nostrils would force him to partly close his eyes and form wrinkles on his forehead. Once the ritual of lighting the 'cigarette' was over, the puffing continued.

He would continue working in his *shamba* while smoking, dawn to dusk. Another peculiar habit that he was known for, was taking of pap with yogurt early in the morning. As it was in several homes those days yogurt was served in a mug made from bamboo. Mwanndimi's capability to till a large portion of a *shamba* in a single day was always the talk of the village. He was a standard setter when it came to tilling a *shamba*. Many a youth dreamt of becoming like him some day.

Another person that I remember was Mwelu. He was disabled and an albino. He came to our home once in a while. Whenever he came I would hide myself. My mother would prepare some food for him. I later came to learn that he was a Jehovah Witness also known as *abasisimikisi* because they were said to insist on the Word of God, from the Bible. He came to our home to visit one of my grandfathers, also a Jehovah Witness faithful; he was sick.

Also in my memory is the man who was known as Mwakinyomosya. He was so much attached to his donkey that you could not imagine seeing him without the beast. When the man died, so it was said, the donkey cried at his grave. He used to ride his donkey majestically. He was not concerned about the other users of the footpaths.

The sight of him was enough to scare me. But even adults seemed to be afraid of him. I was so afraid of him that when he passed it was as if everything lost life, even the wind. The branches stopped dancing and birds stopped singing. With the man around, the village seemed a very unsafe place. And he was around a lot, having particularly come to enjoy the local brew at the village *pombe* shop.

One day my mother and I were walking from a milling machine. She balanced a basket full of maize flour on her head. I was walking by her side. Both of us did not realize that Mwakinyomosya was riding his donkey just behind us. He rode the donkey so close to my mother. Thanks to a woman who was walking in the opposite direction. She saw the move. She screamed a warning to my mother *ejoo*! My mother stepped aside. She could have fallen down. Mwakinyomosya was unconcerned. I looked at him. He was in white pith helmet, white coat and gum boots. I clung to my mother so both of us moved slowly.

The incident happened near a *pombe* shop. There were men drinking in the open air section of the shop. They continued drinking or rather they pretended to be drinking. No one showed concern over what had just happened to us. I didn't believe that they had not seen what had happened. Some lifted the bowl shaped calabashes of *pombe* to their mouths. They did this to cover their faces. None uttered a word of sympathy to my mother nor raised their concern against Mwakinyomosya's behaviour.

There was also Bwite, a "superman" of his time. At the *pombe* shop nobody dared joke with him. It was rumoured that he was so strong that he could beat any number of men. It was alleged that he once jumped from a third floor of the cooperative society building, while running from being arrested by policemen. People believed that he acquired strength by medicine he got from a distant land.

Whenever Bwite came to the *pombe* shop word would spread around. My peers and I would go near the place. We would hang just to see if he would start a fight. But I never saw him fighting. Nevertheless I believed that he was a "superman". My father did not want me to go near the *pombe* shop but I did anyway. My friends and I knew that after taking beer people were not very careful with their things so we combed the area every morning. During one of those "ventures" I picked up a wristwatch. I immediately headed home, laughing all the way. That was how one of uncles on my father's side discovered the secret. He asked me to give him the watch fooling me that it was not working properly and he could repair it. I did so. When I reached home I narrated the incident to my mother.

"Why did he take it? It was you who was lucky enough see it and pick it up," she shouted. Then, she turned towards the direction of my uncle's home and she asked me to follow her. She walked hurriedly while I ran behind her. She was able to get the watch from my uncle. He did not resist. I believe he didn't resist because he respected my mother as his sister in law. I later examined the watch. It was white with words "Roma" behind the glass screen. I kept looking at the watch all the way home.

Before such evenings when we hung near the *pombe* shop, we would spend some of the afternoons at Lina stream. The water stream was diverted from its natural course using bamboo poles. The bamboo "pipes" were connected in such a way that they extend to a certain length and let out the water at a height of about seven feet. That was the place from where we took bath. It was famous as *salala*. There was a *salala* for men and another for women. As children we loved taking bath at the *salala*. We would wash then smear ourselves with mud then wash again then smear again until we were fed up of the game.

There was a big rock beside the *salala*. We would spread ourselves on the rock, like lizards. This way we enjoyed the sunshine. We even had a 'lullaby' to persuade the sun not to go away:

Ungajongaga ngwangu
Ngukupa ni fumbi ngwangu.

Don't go away my dearest
I will even give you an egg.

After taking bath we wandered around the uncultivated patches of land along the stream looking for wild fruits: guavas, *manyore* berries, *mangulungulu* and many others. Sometimes we hunted for underground honey. This was a wonderful honey made by *utupasi* smaller bees that did not sting. To get the honey of the insect we had to locate a tiny hole on the ground. Once we found one, we would dig around it with a stick and wow! There would be a lot of honey under there.

Some days it would happen that I would be at home most of the time. I would see visitors coming to our home. Often visitors were my mother's close relatives from Ilalabwe. Car transport from the village to the market in Tukuyu was rare. So, on their way to or from the market they would pass at home, 'refuel 'and proceed with the rest of the journey. During the stop over my mother would hurriedly prepare a mountain of *ugali* and soup of roasted groundnuts grounded on *ulwala*, a grinding stone.

I would be around when the visitors ate *ugali*. I admired their art of eating. In a typical scene a man would pick with his fingers, a big chunk of *ugali* from the "foot of *ugali* Mountain." Moving his fingers like a master of pottery at work, he would mould a king size ball of *ugali*. Then with his mid finger he would divide it into two medium size balls. Using his thumb he would push the ball in front to the tip of his index finger. Then with his thumb he would press the ball in the middle. The ball would look like a soupspoon. The "spoon" enabled him to scoop a reasonable amount of soup for blending the ball. Then the two, perfectly blended to proportion, would be hurled into the mouth. His hand would not move for another chunk until the previous ball has gone through the Adam's apple. Nothing would be done in a hurry. Gradually but confidently the "mountain" in the plate would be leveled.

One day I stared at a visitor while he was eating. "Why do you stare at him? That is bad manner," my mother rebuked. "Don't rebuke him, all kids are like that," the visitor said with a ball of *ugali* in his mouth. I walked out.

CHAPTER 2

THE BUSH SCHOOL AND KISWAHILI

The "movement order" that I should go to stay with my uncle in the Precious Stone Town came when I was a pupil at Bujinga Bush School in the village. I can't remember how many classrooms were there but I remember we had two teachers. They were Jacob and Richard. Jacob would be in a white shirt, white shorts, white stockings and black shoes. And he was the head teacher. Richard would be in a coat and a cap. I envied Jacob in that appearance and position. "When I grow up I would be a teacher and dress like Jacob," I thought.

The building was constructed using bamboo poles. The roof was thatched. We sat on benches made of bamboo. There were no desks. Writing was possible by crossing our legs. The thigh would serve as a desk. With our exercise books on our thighs we learned to write. A car tyre ring rim served as a bell. In the morning while getting prepared to go to school I would have my ears attentive to the bell ring. The morning bell ring signified the beginning of inspection parade. The echo of the ring would engulf the ridges. When I heard the ring before leaving home I knew that I was late. Being late was punishable by strokes of a cane. I feared to be beaten. My mother tells me that I would always hurriedly prepare and leave for school.

Before we entered into the classrooms there was the inspection parade. The school band played the inspection song. The instruments of the school band consisted of a big drum, two small cylindrical drums and four pipes made of bamboo. The band boys would play and Richard would be standing attentively beside them. "*Pumba tupu* it is all rubbish," he would rebuke to them.

The rest of us would be standing in a straight line. The teacher on duty would pass from one line to another. As the teacher inspected nails, hair, teeth, shirts, shorts, and buttons we stood in awe. We feared most when the teacher on duty ordered us to remove our shirts so that he could inspect our backs.

If the teacher suspected that one had a dirty back, he would instruct him (the school at that time had no girl pupils) to raise his shirt over his shoulder, then he (the teacher) would rub the back with his finger. Those found with layers of deposited dirt would be thrown out of the parade. The prefects would be instructed to take them to the *salala*. One day in June, I was among those who had to go to the *salala*. While there the prefect took a handful of fine sand from the stream bed. He mixed it with soap foam and rubbed my back. "There is a layer of dirty. When did you last take bath?" He asked. "Last week. It is so cold these days," I replied, shyly. "When you take bath at the *salala* next time, ask someone to rub your back. Now your back is clean enough. Put on your clothes and let's go."

But some pupils did not return to school after being found dirty or beaten for being late. Then one day, I saw some prefects near our home. "What are they looking for?" I asked my mother. "I don't know," she replied. Later I found out that the prefects were looking for my father's half brother. He had not been to school for sometimes. The prefects were sent by teachers to carry out the "operation". Later on when the truants were back to school, we booed by the song that I cannot remember but close to this one:

Asiyependa shule mjinga kabisa

One who does not like the school is very ignorant

Akipata barua atembeza kutwa

When he gets a letter he takes it around the whole day, looking for someone to read for him.

The language of instruction at the bush school was Kiswahili. But outside the classroom we did not speak much of the language. Even in the village we did not speak Kiswahili but Kinyakyusa, our mother language. Other people in the village mostly spoke Kinyakyusa too. I have a feeling that my people did not have the enthusiasm to learn Kiswahili because the traders could understand as well as speak Kinyakyusa. The only community that seemed to speak good Kiswahili was the one we called Waswahili. They lived in town and they were traders like Indians, Arabs and Somalis. But the Waswahili were particularly known for making and selling: buns, chapattis and other local bites *vitumbua* and *bagia*. They had boys who worked for them. The boys walked around the market place and the main bus stand selling the stuff. Often, the boys came from other places far from the villages around but after living with the Waswahili for a certain period they also became good speakers of Kiswahili.

Thus the people in Tukuyu town were of different origins. But it did not ring in my mind that the Indians, the Arabs, the Somalis and the Waswahili were not natives. To me it was as if they had always been there. They were supposed to be in town and we were supposed to be in the village. They were supposed to run businesses and we were supposed to farm. That was it. The villagers went into town during the day and returned to the village in the evening. And the Waswahili were rarely seen in the village.

From the Bush school and the interaction with Waswahili, though not much, I learnt some Kiswahili. I could for instance correctly answer to the question "*Jina lako nani*, what is your name?" "*Jina langu* Felo, my name is Felo," I would answer.

Then one morning, my father told me that I had to go to a Precious Stone Town in the north and stay with my uncle, the brother of my mother. I remember him saying in a low voice, "Fellowes, you will go to stay with your uncle in Precious Stone Town." "What about the schooling?" I raised the point as an excuse. "You will find a better school there. The Bush school is not good enough. We asked your uncle if there would be a better school there. Last week we received his letter saying indeed there is a very nice school there and that he would be waiting for you," he replied. I could not imagine life outside the village far away from home. I could also not imagine life without my father, my mother and my brother Daniel. "I will not go," I said while crying.

My father repeated the message in his sternest voice and I yielded. Helena, my mother's younger sister had arrived the previous day. I was happy to have her with us. It was not until that morning that I knew that she came purposely to take me to Ilalabwe, ready for the journey to Precious Stone Town through Mbeya and Itigi.

My father woke me up in the morning. We had breakfast together. Whenever it came into my mind that I would soon be leaving I sobbed. Then we started the journey to

Ilalabwe on foot. I looked my father, my mother and Daniel. They stood looking at me. I realized they were not going to join me even in the first part of the journey. I broke into tears. Helena held my hand and kind of dragged me. The journey to Precious Stone Town had begun.

CHAPTER 3

MY FIRST SAFARI

On the day of my departure from Ilalabwe, Helena, woke me up in the morning. She, my grandmother and I walked on foot to the bus stop.

I was six years old and the bus stop was five kilometres away. Helena, who was to accompany me to Shinyanga, only supported me when it came to crossing slippery "bridges" - actually a log laid on the two banks of a stream or river. At such places, she would carry me on her back.

There was only one bus operating between Tukuyu and Mbeya at that time. It was owned by an Indian businessman. When the bus arrived that morning, the three of us boarded. There were other passengers but the bus was not full. I sat by the window. This was my first experience travelling by bus. The bus did not seem to be moving but the banana trees on both sides of the road did. We arrived at Mbeya terminal in the afternoon. We had to proceed to the terminal for the EAR&H buses. They were the only buses operating on the Mbeya – Itigi route, a distance of about 500 kilometres of a road without tarmac.

There were two bus drivers. They were in khaki uniforms and caps. They looked older than my father.

When the bus was ready to leave I looked out through the window and I saw my grandma. She was sitting under a big tree. Somehow, for reasons I cannot explain, I felt sorry for her. Although seven years later I met her at her home in Ilalabwe, it is that image of her sitting under the tree on that day in December 1965 that is fresh in my mind.

The bus left. It drove as if going back to Tukuyu, then it turned right. It went through the snake-like corner at Isanga and the Kawetere forest reserve. We then passed Chunya, Makongorosi, Lupatingatinga, Kipembawe, Kambikatoto and Rungwa game reserve.

We also crossed river Lupatingatinga.

The river was famous for its alluvial gold. It brought down the crumbs of the yellowish mineral from the hills beyond. Men from Tukuyu who rushed to the place to seek their fortune were said to have gone to dig gold, *ibwe*.

The road was bumpy and the ride was uncomfortable especially for those of us who were on the back seats. Often we were thrown up nearly hitting the inner part of the roof. One man sitting on the front seat turned to ask those of us in the back "the drive is asking if he should reduce the speed?" We readily agreed, *"eee tata,"* that we would very much appreciate it if the driver would slow down. Then it turned out that the man had not talked to the drive. He only meant to tease us. The driver did not slow down.

It was past midnight when the bus stopped suddenly. We had not yet reached Itigi, we were still within the forest of Rungwa game reserve. The driver disembarked from the bus and the passengers too. With the headlights of the bus still on, I could see an animal lying in front of the bus. It had some blood oozed from its mouth and looked dead.

The animal was not among the big five, but it could not be said to be small. I heard some passengers saying that the driver must be a very lucky person because "The animal is a sign of good fortune." I saw the driver draw a knife. He cut part of the nose and the nails of the front legs. A few other passengers also did so. They said if one possessed them luck would be on their way.

After about twenty minutes we rode off. We arrived at Itigi early in the morning. After washing we went for tea at a kiosk near the station. Tea was served in glasses instead of cups. It looked milky and tasted salty. It was not like the one my father prepared at home. After tea we walked around.

For the first time since I had started the journey I noticed a big difference between where I was and home. Itigi was dry and dusty. Apart from a few trees, that seemed exotic, at the railway station the place was bare. The white soil lay there bare without grass. Thus the wind blew freely. It threw the white dust on faces of people. So everyone had a pale face. The tree leaves and flowers released a scent with which I was not comfortable. I also saw, for the first time, people begging. I realized that they were blind. They had black clothes wrapped around their bodies. Men and women had the same clothes. It was not like home where a man would wear a shirt and a pair of trousers while a woman would wear a gown.

I lost the enthusiasm to travel any farther. I wanted to return home. Why in the first place did my father want me to live away from our village? I felt unsafe and uprooted. I wondered why my father should do such a bad thing to me. Why should he deprive me of all the good things at home? I looked down the road that we drove on from Mbeya. It was so straight. I could see to the horizon. I didn't feel all the distance we had travelled. Home was like somewhere just behind the horizon. It was like I could go on foot.

"I want to go home," I told Helena. Tears rolled down my cheeks.

"Are you a fool? Can't you see that the bus has left already? How would you go back?" I sobbed. "Stop weeping lest you become a fool, *akuja ndema,*" she kind of barked.

I stopped weeping to prove that I was not a fool, though I still felt the desire to go home.

When everybody seemed to be silent and waiting for something to happen, I heard the sound of a whistle. The sound was not very loud and clear. It sounded like someone suffering from asthma who was struggling to breathe. It was a hissing sound. I observed that many people, who were at the station, turned their heads eastward. I also looked eastward. I heard some people say the train was coming. The big black engine of the train, facing east, was like a provoked bull charging towards the station. The closer it got to the station the more its 'temper' cooled down. Then a man, who undoubtedly was one of the Railway staff, threw a token carrier with something tied to it. The driver caught it and he threw to the staff on the ground another token carrier. Thus they exchanged the carriers. The man caught the carrier with the same mastery as the driver had done. I was impressed with the mastery of both in throwing and catching the token carriers. But what was the meaning of the whole thing. The train then halted. It was no longer like a charging bull. It was friendly and it seemed to invite people on board.

Six years later I came to see the film about the construction of the Mombassa to Kampala railway. In that film the Indian labourers, under European supervisors were involved in the risky hard work. There were no machines used in the construction work. The labourers carried the rails on their shoulders from one point to the next.

But the most difficult situation arose at the Tsavo stretch. Lions came at night and snatched labourers from the camp. In one of the notable scenes in the film, one of the engineers was picked by a lioness from a wagon. He was sitting in the wagon with his rifle. He was actually trying to protect himself and fellow workers who were in the wagon. He remained awake for a long time but the lioness did not appear. Then he got tired. His eye lids were heavy with drowsiness. Occasionally he yawned and struggled to keep himself awake. But eventually drowsiness overpowered him. He fell asleep. The lioness appeared a short moment after he had fallen asleep. With her paws firmly placed on the window of the wagon, the lioness stretched herself upward. She held him by the neck. He woke up from his sleep with his eyes protruded. He looked panicky and helpless. The lioness pulled the poor fellow through the window. Despite these difficulties the railway reached Kampala. The first steam engine train to arrive in Kampala whistled as it approached the station. The Indian labourers were overwhelmed with joy. They danced and sang. Some of them moved swiftly and sat on the bar in front of the engine. It was like they were holding a tamed bull by the horns.

When we boarded, that year when I was six years, we would be seated on seats made with wooden bases. It was 11.00 when we boarded the train at Itigi. As it pulled away, the train did not seem to move so much as swing.

Before we arrived at the next station a man in khaki uniform approached us for tickets. I heard some of the passengers saying that he was a T.T. Later I came to learn the actual job title was Travelling Ticket Examiner (TTE). The TTE looked smart in his uniform: a white shirt and a tie, a khaki coat and trousers. The buttons of his coat, like those of the conductor of the bus that we travelled by from Mbeya, was engraved with letters EAR&H. He had a thick beard and a turban tightly wound around his head. My aunt presented our tickets to him. He examined and punched them with a nipper. He then proceeded to do the same with other passengers.

We arrived at Tabora Station at 1900. The train remained at the station for several hours. I heard some passengers say the reason for the delay was that the engine had to be filled with water. During this time we remained in our seats, we were afraid other passengers would sit on them if we disembarked, even for a short moment.

Before the train departed I heard an announcement from loud speakers fixed on the roof of one of the buildings. *Tafadhali sikilizeni, tafadhali sikilizeni. Garimoshi ya kwenda Mwanza iko njia moja. Abiria wote mnaombwa kuingia ndani.* "Attention please, attention please, the train to Mwanza is now ready for departure. All passengers are advised to get on board." The voice of the announcer was heavy, polite and clear. I didn't get tired of listening to him. Then the train slowly moved from the station and gained momentum.

We arrived at Shinyanga town and we proceeded to a small town called Mapozeo. I learned that entrance to the Precious Stone Town was restricted because of the mining activities. Entrance was allowed by passes issued by the township authority, which was why we spent a night at Mapozeo while my

uncle was processing our passes. We spent a
night at Mapozea in a guest house. It was at
the guesthouse that I heard people talking a
different language from ours. And some had
their ears pierced. I was scared of them. At
night I slept very close to Helena.

After spending the night at Mapozeo we
proceeded to the Precious Stone Town. Our
passes were not ready yet so we had to spend
another night at a rest house opposite the
town's main gate. My aunt, the wife of my
uncle, was there to meet us. She led Helena
to the part of the rest house for women and
she led me to the men side. I found that
unlike the guest house at Mapozeo, this one
had electricity and water taps.

In the room I was to stay, there was another
guest. He did not have pierced ears and he
greeted me kindly. In the afternoon my aunt
brought *ugali* for me. She also welcomed
the man to eat with me. His eating manner
was strange to me. Instead of starting at the
foot of the *ugali* 'mountain', like the men at
home, he started at the top. And hardly had
he swallowed the first ball than he picked a
piece of meat from the bowl. He nibbled it
and placed what remained of it on the very
spot where he had scooped the *ugali* ball.

The piece of meat on top was still dripping wet with the soup. That way, the 'white mountain' of *ugali* got soiled. My appetite went down because of his eating manners, though I was still hungry.

"So the next meal I would not be eating with this man," I thought and felt relieved.

In the afternoon the passes were ready. We proceeded to the town gate that was manned by policemen.

CHAPTER 4

THE GOOD AND THE ODD

My aunt led the way to the police desk, Helena and I trailed behind her. Seeing the police officer in his khaki uniform my muscle became tense. It was like coming face to face with the tax collector in the home village. My heart thumped. I stood by Helena. In a while the check was over; we went through the passage. I relaxed. The fence that made the passage was behind me but I was still inside the fence that surrounded the whole of Precious Stone Town. Much later I would learn that the town was unique in the whole country in that it was the only place where one could not just enter without a pass. The reason for restricted entrance was to protect the precious stones mined there.

I joined my uncle and his immediate family in Block E. My uncle had two daughters, Tupokigwe and Isengela. Neither of them had started school. During my early days in the town, my uncle noticed that I was home sick. Sometimes he would find me crying for no obvious reason. He bought a sweet for me every day. He would bring the sweet when he returned home from work at five in the evening. With time I stopped thinking about home. I became part of the family and part of the children of Changanyiko.

I got acquainted to other boys in our block. We formed a football team. The team played with other teams in other blocks, A to M. Each block had twenty houses arranged in five columns and four rows. From one house to another, column wise, there was a distance of about twenty metres and row-wise fifteen metres. Each house had two apartments, each for one family. An apartment consisted of two rooms and a kitchen.

Each ten-house block shared toilet facilities and a place for washing clothes and dishes. The washing place was like a large dining table made of concrete. Then taps, about four of them fixed on each side. Toddlers were also bathed at the washing "table". On one side of the "table" there was a place for washing dishes. So the common scenario was that of women, standing on both sides of the 'table', washing clothes, dishes and toddlers. I helped my aunt washing dishes. Washing dishes with women all over the place was difficult for me. So I washed the dishes as quickly as I could. In that way I did not do the washing properly and as a result my aunt rebuked me.

One day Tupokigwe was on the "washing table" and she wanted to get down. I wanted to prove that I was strong enough to carry her and get her on the ground. I opened my arm and she kind of landed on my chest. I felt her weight. We went down together. The women and children around burst into laughter. I gathered myself up and lifted her from the ground. We went home. I was glad that she did not report the incident to my aunt. After that incident whenever I went to the washing table I felt shy before the women for I thought they would be talking about me.

I also hated the washing place because it was frequently blocked by food leftovers. And the bins by the washing place, meant for the food leftovers, were always full and released bad odour. I even felt in a more of unpleasant situation because the washing place was close to the latrines. The latrines were routinely cleaned by the so called *Wachura*, normally around ten in the morning. But the cleanliness lasted for a few hours. By two in the afternoon they would be in bad shape. They were actually pit latrines. But there were those people who did not use the appropriate places to relieve themselves. They just released excreta on the floor. Thus there were hours of the day when the heaps of excreta were all over the floor. It was a situation that provoked a nauseous feeling. It was not a place you would like to go after a meal. Thus I conditioned myself of going to toilet before lunch, at half past twelve.

The sewerage system was centralized so the blocks were not littered with cesspit tanks. Between the rows and columns of houses, there wasn't a single tree or flower plant. Each house was supplied with electricity from underground cables. In front of each house there was a dustbin, about the size of two twenty-litre capacity buckets, for solid waste. Every Thursday a truck passed from block to block to collect waste. The waste was taken to a dumping site. Some children from Changanyiko scavenged at the dump and picked things.

The truck that passed to collect solid

waste was one of those things that excited us children in Changanyiko. It was a special truck designed to compact the bulk waste thrown inside. In that way, it carried a lot of waste. Trailing behind the truck and looking at how it squeezed the waste was one of the things we did, especially during school holidays.

The driver of the truck became very popular among children. His name was David. I liked his name because it was similar to a character in an English class reader. The book was about one David who, one day entered into a vehicle that had been parked close to his school. The driver was not around and David dared drive the vehicle away.

On a certain Thursday, my friend Sta and I asked David to take us along on his waste collecting truck. I looked at David, his hands held the steering wheel. It didn't seem to be difficult for him except when he engaged a gear. His left hand became tense, the veins more visible. I heard a rattling sound whenever he engaged the gear. We also saw children playing, women moving here and there. We enjoyed exploring one location after another, from block E to M. But the truck did not drive into Uzunguni, Uhindini, bachelor quarters.

I knew that all white people lived in Uzunguni. I also knew that Bapu, one of our teachers lived in Uhindini. Bapu was especially known for wearing a white shirt, white shorts and white socks. He taught Science in Standard Seven. Pupils admired him for catching butterflies and snakes for the science laboratory. Our Headmaster also lived in Uhindini area.

I was also aware that Baba Richard a white family friend and who happened to be my uncle's supervisor lived in Uzunguni. Whenever I saw him, he was dressed in a pair of khaki shorts, socks and safari boots. He smoked a cigar. I heard my uncle explaining to aunt that Baba Richard had worked at Kimberly in South Africa before he came to Tanzania.

Baba Richard and his family expressed their friendliness towards ours in different ways. They would send us gifts from time to time, especially during Christmas. On one such occasion, 1969 Christmas, I received a beautiful Tee-shirt, a hat and a pair of safari boots from Richard. I was very happy. I put them on and went to the Sunday school class. All who were there admired my new look. So, it was with pride and affection we would introduce Baba Richard and his family to our neighbours in Block E as "our white man, *mzungu wetu*." Not many White workers at the Precious Stone Town visited the Changanyiko area. Therefore, whenever Baba Richard drove up to our residence in his silver 109 Model Land Rover all children in the neighbourhood would flock to our house. "Is this your white man, *huyu ndiyo mzungu wenu?*" they would ask me. "Yes. What about you? Who is your white man?" Though I knew that Baba Richard lived in Uzunguni and Bapu lived in Uhindini I had no idea how the houses looked like inside.

One morning, though, coming from a Sunday school class I visited a relative in Uhindini. The house had within it a toilet and a bathroom with water taps. The kitchen had a washing sink and a water tap as well. In the living room there were two pairs of sofa sets. While there were no tree on the Changanyiko 'rows' and 'columns', the avenues, lanes and *cul-de-sac* of Uhindini had shade trees, fruit trees and flowers. We sometimes sneaked into Uhindini to pick guavas. In one of such incident, one of us from Changanyiko was caught by one of the residents. He had picked three guavas. The owner asked the boy either to leave them or accept three slaps as the price for the guava. The bay accepted the three slaps.

Next to Uhindini lay Uzunguni where I was particularly fascinated by the Exclusive Club's lawn tennis court, a swimming pool and a golf course. One of the things I liked was to stand near the golf course and gaze at a tractor mowing grass.

But otherwise, I would spent my evening time on a veranda of our home in Block E, Changanyiko, with Sta, one of my playmates and tell stories to each other. The story I would tell was the one that Azizi had told me at school. We had just been enrolled for Standard One and Aziz was the first boy at school I got acquainted with. Aziz encouraged me when my oversize shorts were embarrassing me. He advised me to roll it on the waist. I took his advice and the shorts were adjusted to size. From that day we moved around together especially during break time. It was during one of the break times that Aziz told me a story of a big snake which was drawn out of Lake Victoria in Mwanza. He said that a long time ago his grandpa was a seaman of a ship in the lake. One day, his grandpa and other seamen saw, at a great distance, chains descending from the sky and sinking into the water. After a while a big snake, bound by the chains emerged from the water.

After the story from Aziz, Sta, shared with me his experience of visiting Mwanza. He and his parents had been there. His father was on leave. He said Mwanza was a big town with many cars and people. He also told us about a wonder shaving machine. He said the machine was like a big hat. The barber's job was simply to place it properly on your head and in a few minutes it was done in the style you wished. Thereafter, I started dreaming of visiting Mwanza.

When it came to songs Sta was not short of one. He taught me two songs. I quickly learnt them even though I did not understand what they actually meant. They were used especially during the hide-and-seek game. The first song was:

Saka saka nanga
Dia dia kompo
Kompo la Magigina
Madalimung a bu.

The other one was:

Bosi tandala tema na mungangala wamonile
hondela ni Makoyokoyo madalimunga bu.

One morning were sitting on the veranda and Sta said: "If you eat a lot of pawpaw you would discharge faeces red in colour." He added that he himself had a proof to that. I wanted to know from where he got the pawpaw. He said he had picked them from the Company garden.

I was tempted by this story. We went to the Company garden. The place was quiet, nobody seemed to be around. I plucked one big pawpaw. I held it in my hands. It was big and ripe.

Suddenly, my friends started running. I looked back and I saw the gardener running towards us. He was tall, of a dark complexion and strong. Even though he wore gumboots, he could run without difficult. I was gripped with fear, but I did not let the big pawpaw go. I held it firmly and I attempted to run.

Looking behind, I saw the man coming after me. Sta and the others had vanished. His forehead was full of wrinkles and his lips tightened. He did not utter a word but it was as if he was saying: "If I get you, you will be sorry." As I ran, I kept throwing my eyes over my shoulder to see if he was getting nearer. In so doing, I stumbled on a big cabbage and went falling down. The man got me. I was lying there begging for mercy. I was trembling desperately. He grabbed my right hand and forced me up. I stood up with my head slightly above his waist. Standing close to me he barked: "Why did you do it?" I was tongue-tied. His face was expression less. I could neither read his feelings nor predict his next move. "Why did you do it," he asked again. "Please forgive me," I replied whilst panting. I felt like energy had been drawn out of my legs. I could neither stand properly nor run away. "It is not me but that other boy," I said with a bit of stammer.

Many years later, I would read Dale Carnegie's *How to Win Friends and Influence People*. In this book Carnegie presents a case of two notorious criminals who are not ready to carry the blame. This is something that turns to be the first reaction among human beings: denying and deflecting.

Unexpectedly, the gardener let me go with the pawpaw. He did not slap me. He warned me not to repeat the act. This was to have a big impact on me. Since then I have been afraid of thieving.

I took the direction that my friends had taken. When I reached the boundary of the garden, I saw Sta. We looked at each other then we laughed. We went to a safe place and ate the big pawpaw. It was red and very delicious.

That specific evening we went to a cinema show at the People's Centre. We liked the cinema because it showed cow boys we pronounced *makaboi*, fighting with pistols and fists. The most celebrated hero was John Wayne but we pronounced: *Joni Waine*. We also called him *mwamba* and anyone who fought against him *jambazi*. "Me *Joni Waine*," I would tell my play mates. But my playmates too shouted back "me *mwamba*". Nobody wanted to be *jambazi*. When the cinema ended the crowd would disperse in groups. Being in a group was important for one's 'security'. There was a baobab tree between the cinema ground and blocks D and E. It was said that there was a *jinni* at the tree and people were afraid to pass there alone. The baobab tree was not the only place where individuals feared to pass on their own. To me the baobab tree was like *pabusisya* forest in my home village.

Some days the people in our block gathered to sing traditional songs from their tribes. They did in turn. I was in the group with my aunt and other members of Wanyakyusa, our ethnic group, and we had this song:

Twisile
Twisile twe bana ba Tukuju
Twisile
Twisile twe bana ba Tukuju
Mwe Jouswe,
Mwapilika akapango.

We have come
We have come, we children of Tukuyu
We have come
We have come, we children of Tukuyu
We are the ones
You must have heard our story.

I became aware of other tribal groups Washashi, Waha, Wanyamwezi, Wanyiramba and Wasumbwa. They came up with their songs. I felt life was so nice that evening. I liked the songs sung by Wanyamwezi. They had many women than men in their group and their voices were fine for me. The Waha had few words in their songs, but they had a lot of vigorous body movements.

But all was not well in Changanyiko, one morning, on my way to school I saw many people around the house of one of our neighbours. The man was on leave and travelled to another town leaving behind three school girls. One of the girls was surrounded by people.

"I don't know how he came in. I just saw him by my bed," she said to the silent crowd.

"The man is one of our neighbours. He wanted to … me and I said no," she said amid sobs.

"He said that he will give me eighty cents if I would let him…. I said no."

"Then he drew a knife. I grabbed it and he pulled it." She burst crying.

I saw the deep wound on her fingers. I felt a cold chill running through my body. I was kind of paralysed. From the explanation of the girls, I could figure out who the man was. He seemed older than my father. "How could a man of that age do such a cruel thing?' I wondered.

Later in the day she came to school and reported the matter to the headmaster. Teachers and pupils were interested to know what happened. She had to repeat the story many times. I heard the headmaster telling her go, mama, go. They should not delay you, *nenda mama nenda wasikucheleweshe*. The girl walked out of the school compound. I stared at her until she disappeared from my sight.

On another school day, I saw the girl with a bandaged hand. She told me that she got the treatment at the main hospital. The mention of the hospital made me remember the bad times there. I had been admitted to the hospital about a month earlier on a malaria case. I was given some pills to swallow. On the third day I felt better except for the itching and it was even serious at night when the lights were off and the ward was dead quiet when all patients were asleep. With the itching I could not fall asleep. There was only one patient who I could see was not asleep as well. He had long beard and he was of a very light complexion. He put on the bedside lamp. He ate his food. It looked like vegetable. After that he combed his beard. It seemed as if there was nobody else in the ward. I felt I like I were not in the world of the living. I was afraid. I blamed the itching for robbing me a sleep. I did not know that the chloroquine pill I had taken was the source of the itching problem. I suspected that something was wrong with the sheets. I rolled the sheets to the end of the bed but the problem did not stop. In the morning, my uncle came to see me. He took me to the bathroom. The warm water gave me some relief. But when I came out at the water the itching resumed.

I was told that I would be discharged that same morning. After the doctor's round my aunt came. She brought me a cake and a soda. The cake was delicious. When it came to soft drinks I only took Fanta. Back in the village my father had instructed me not to take any drink except Fanta and tea. He suspected that any black drink (except tea) had alcohol and drinking it would be a sin.

I had another experience of being hospitalized. Doctors recommended that some of my teeth had to be removed. I was told that I was to be operated. For the operation to take place I was advised not to eat anything in the morning.

The following morning I was taken to the hospital by Mama Masozi, a family friend. My uncle went to his workplace and my aunt had travelled to Tukuyu. The assistant doctor asked me if I had taken something. I said yes. He repeated the question. I told him that I had taken tea with a slice of bread. He told Mama Masozi to take me home and bring me the next day before I take some food. We went home and Mama Masozi insisted on what the assistant doctor had said.

I was taken to the hospital on the second day and the operation was done. I was taken into the theatre. There were three or four people inside. Something like a dust mask was placed on my face. It covered my nose and mouth. There seemed to be some gas coming from a pipe connected to it. I inhaled the gas. They asked me something I did not understand. Then I saw some going out and only Dr Weiti remained. When I woke up I was in the male ward. Mama Masozi was trying to make me eat some porridge. The porridge tasted like the gas I inhaled in the theatre. I saw a 'NO FOOD' sign hanged on two beds opposite mine. I knew the bed occupants were theatre bound.

CHAPTER 5

NOT SELECTED VERSUS FAILED

Unlike the bell at Bujinga Bush School, the bell of the Precious Stone Town Primary School was not an old ring rim of a car wheel, but an electric one. The school messenger was also the timekeeper. He just pressed a button located near the headmaster's office and *griiiii* it went signalizing the start or end of a period.

I especially recall the period when I acted a play in Standard III B organized by our class mistress. I cannot recall her name but what is still fresh in my mind is her smartness. She was always in well groomed colourful dresses which matched well with her complexion. Sometimes she would appear in one type of dress in the morning and another type in the afternoon. Her voice, which seemed to be between nasal and palatal, further distinguished her in that sense.

Besides being a class mistress, she conducted reading lessons. Some of the readings were plays and in such cases she appointed some of us to act before the class. In one of the plays, that I was appointed to act, the story was about a crown that had to be carried from a goldsmith to a king in another country. The critical episode was that the people who were to carry the crown were likely to be attacked and robbed on the way. She gave us instructions on how she thought we could act the play. We practised the play for some time. When she thought that we were ready, she invited Standard III A to the audience. The pupils of the two classes squeezed alongside one another in one classroom. It was "full house" when we went on "the stage". I carried the 'crown'. It was actually a green hat with white embroidery. The hat was among the presents my family received from Baba Richard. Before the cheering audience "we successfully delivered the crown to the king despite the ambush on the highway".

Standard IV however, was not easy for me. I especially had hard time with the teacher who taught us English. He would sit on his chair behind a table, as big as a dining one, in front of the class and from there each of us to read a sentence or two. I could not properly pronounce the word "us." Instead I pronounced it as if it were a Kiswahili word. Thus it sounded *"usi."* He beat me with a stick and asked me to read again. *"Usi,"* I pronounced. "Monica, read the same sentence," he asked the girl who sat next to me. *"Ahs,"* Monica pronounced. "Good, Monica. Now Fellowes, it is your turn read the word," he said loudly. *"Usi,"* I said in a choked voice. He beat me with a stick and asked Monica to read again for me. Monica had it correct. "Okay Fellowes read," he barked. *"Usi,"* I said. He didn't ask me to read anymore. I hated English and I hated the teacher too.

Later in 1970, while in Standard V we were introduced to carpentry and fine art. In the carpentry workshop we learned things like cross joints, dove joint, tenon saw, rip saw, mallet, file and other things. I paid more interest in fine art than carpentry.

In the fine art class we learned how to use brush in painting and how to make pots and cups from clay. Well painted pictures were pasted on the wall. I painted a picture of two men facing each other. I painted them in white gowns and fezzes. The picture was my impression of two men playing *bao*. The picture was pasted on the wall. We also learnt how to shade a picture after drawing by free hand. It was in the fine art class where I increased my awareness that things look big when they are near and look small when they are far. In the fine art class this was called perspective. I also learned that the horizon was the farthest point the eyes could see. The lesson therefore shattered the myth I held during my childhood that the horizon was where the earth met the blue sky. In a landscape picture hills in the horizon, would be painted in blue colour. This would give the impression as if they were really far from the viewer.

It was from the lessons of that class that I could draw good pictures using a crayon. I could not paint properly with brush. So I admired the way our teacher using the brush with ease. He painted very nice pictures. "Where did he learn to paint?" We repeatedly asked one another. "Uganda," someone said.

It was between Standard V and VI, through the Geography subject, that I broadened my view of the world as well. I liked, and many other pupils did, the Geography book: *Do you Know?* Topics in the book included:

Wheat farming in Canada, the railway from Montreal to Vancouver, cotton farming in America, sheep rearing in New Zealand and the Eskimo as the people of Greenland. We read about the igloos, houses made of snow. We were surprised by the life of the Eskimo for we believed that they lived in the igloos.

I was, generally, proud of our school. I could not be compared it with my former school in my village. The school in the mine township was built of concrete blocks, painted and roofed with imported tiles. Each classroom had several windows made of glass panels. On Fridays each pupil was provided with a piece of soap in order to wash school uniforms ready for Monday's parade.

During the morning break each pupil got a half pint of fresh milk from the company's dairy farm. A dairy man in his white coat and black gumboots would bring a crate of bottles of milk right at the door of each classroom. The school had twenty eight classrooms. All of them received crates of milk every day.

Transport was provided for pupils. There were school buses operating different routes: *Changanyiko*, *Uzunguni* and *Uhindini*. Some

teachers also used the buses, but some had
their own cars. The cars models that parked
in front of the school building include
Austin, Peugeot, Anglia, Ford Escort, Morris
and several others. Among those cars, one
fascinated the pupils the most. We did not
know its name. We nick-named it *chura*,
because it looked like a toad. I would later
learn that it was a French model Citroen.
What was interesting about the car was that
its body could be lifted up and lowered down.
Its body was lifted up before it moved and
when it came to a complete stop the body
was lowered somewhat covering its wheels.

In Standard VII when we were about to
do the final examinations, I happened to love
Kipusa. She seemed to possess electric-like
power. Whenever I passed near her, I would
feel a strange current flowing through my
body. I adored her very much but I could not
express my feelings to her. It was, perhaps,
out of desperation that I decided to share
my feelings about Kipusa with Ngalangala.
He was a jovial person and much older than
I. Above all, he always boasted of having
experience. He worked as a houseboy for a
senior bachelor within the Precious Stone
Town.

As I started sharing my feelings about Kipusa, he burst into a loud laughter. "What a coincidence, Kipusa has also been talking nicely about you!" He said. He added that together we could prove her love to me by consulting the "oracle book". The book turned out to be two pages torn from a pupil's exercise book with statements copied and translated from what we believed to be the Napoleonic oracle book. Most of the pupils at our primary school possessed it. Who started the circulation was not known to me. Most copied from their friends.

I let Ngalagala consult the oracle. My heart kept beating fast. My hands shook. Beads of sweat formed on my forehead. I let Ngalangala do everything. After crossing out all similar letters from both names, he established the total number of uncrossed letters. He checked the statement against the number. It read: "*Anakupenda, lakini anaona haya kukuambia*". It translates into: She loves you but she is too shy to admit it to you. I felt good, very good indeed. I imagined a day would come when I would marry her. But would my parents agree to that: she was not from my tribe. After the oracle I had the courage to talk to her and we became friends. I felt good by merely thinking of her. Days seemed to pass very quickly that I didn't even notice that the date for the final examinations was nearing while I was not prepared enough.

We sat for the examinations in September. The examination papers did not include Fine Art subject but English and Mathematics. I was not good in any of these subjects. In the several mathematics tests that we did, it was only one that I scored marks within the average. The day I had the average score our Mathematics teacher commented: "I am afraid I gave you a very simple test that even Fellowes got good marks."

The results for the final examinations were announced sometimes in November. The school administration in posting the results had written: "Those who have been selected to join secondary school their names are listed below." My name was not among those selected. News spread all over the town. And in Changanyiko, where I lived, people talked about pass or fail.

My uncle did not ask me about my results and did not tell him. The two of us remained in that state for a time.

I knew that Kipusa also had not been

selected but I didn't see her as one who had that embarrassment of a "failure". She was as I had always seen her. It was me who had "failed" and not her. I felt belittled by the examination and no longer imagined marrying her.

Completion of Standard Seven at the Precious Stone Town, for those not selected to join secondary school, was followed by three years at a technical school or at the Folk Development School (FDS). I first did the aptitude test for joining the technical school. I and others who came for the test, entered into a room at the school. We were told that there would be a film show from which we should see and learn how to do what we would be given thereafter. The instructions were provided by a person standing behind a projector. 'Carefully look at what the characters in the film do. After the film show you will be asked to do the same', he said amid our deep silence. Then lights went off. There was no other sound in the room except that of the running projector.

It was a silent film in black and white. It was like watching a Charlie Chaplin movie. There were two characters in dark overalls.

Each had a box full of nuts, bolts and several other things. They picked nuts and fixed them to bolts; their hands moved so fast. In about five minutes the film was over. The light went on. In front of me there was a heap of nuts and bolts and an empty box. Then came the instruction 'Fix the nuts to the right bolt and put them in the box', said the man behind the projector. With my hands trembling I started to sort out nuts from the heap and try to find the right bolts. Hardly had I gone half way then a bell rung. Time was over. After two weeks or so the results were announced. I had failed the test.

Then I had another opportunity; to sit for the FDS aptitude test. I sat for the test and after a week or so I went for the results. The results were issued by the Head instructor himself. We were called one by one. The head instructor was known for seriousness. The students of the school said that the man never laughed. I was called in and the head instructor was sitting behind a long executive table. He told me that I had passed the aptitude test and that was all. I went out. After that we were taken around the school buildings and farms. We reached one of the farms and the instructor who took us there told us that it was a commercial farm. "It is ten hectors," the instructor said. It was my first time to hear the word 'commercial'. I did not understand what it meant.

The day ended and we retired to the hostels. We washed and went to the cafeteria at the People's Centre. There was a scramble for food. The bigger boys did not respect the queue. The stronger ate first then others and I followed. Actually, the stronger were not boys but adults. There was one man who was believed to be the strongest. He was simply called *Mzee*. He never stood in a queue. He would come late and just go straight to the food pot and the servers would serve him.

One afternoon one of the bigger boys could not accept this. He asked *Mzee* to follow the queue. *Mzee* was not ready to be 'humiliated' like that. He grabbed the boy ready to 'teach him a lesson'. It turned out to be a fight, which apparently he had not expected and he had underestimated the boy. By instinct he made a quick move but found that he was locked in a wrestling fight. They were like two bulls with their horns locked. Other boys started cheering. Simply, it was not Mzee's day. When the fight was just taking the attention of everybody, *Mzee* was flat on his back with part of his well dressed hair on the floor. He could not help his hair getting soiled by the dirty and wet floor. The filth on the floor consisted of trodden pieces of *ugali*, yogurt and stew. The boys jeered "*Mzee* Usukile Pabandu teach the boy a lesson." But simply it wasn't *Mzee's* day.

It was unbelievable! The boy, David, ran away from the cafeteria. *Mzee* Usukile Pabandu pulled himself up. His wet shorts stuck to his buttocks and the wet shirt stuck to his back. His face wearing shameful expression, he trailed towards the exit. He did not take his lunch that day. And from that day everyone, including *Mzee* Usukile Pabandu stood in the queue.

Mzee was almost the age of my father and my heart didn't accept what had happened to him. But my eyes, ears and mind convinced me that he was a bully. As a bully he deserved what he got.

The scramble for food and the idea of working in the commercial farm, made me dislike FDS. So was happy when my uncle told me that I would have to go back to Tukuyu to repeat Standard VII. He gave me the letter that he received from my father. I read it. From the handwriting I could tell that Daniel must be the one who wrote it. At that time of the year, being a Form Two student at Tabora Secondary School, he must have been on holiday. In the letter, my father insisted that I should go back and repeat Standard VII for he could not see my future through FDS training. I left the town for Tukuyu, my home town in January 1973.

However, the good plan of the Precious Stone Town, as it was at then, has always remained live in my memory: its layout, the management of solid waste, transport services, social facilities, medical care, water, electricity and milk supplies were much better than most of the places I came to know. I will always admire the way things were organised in Precious Stone Town the time I was there, December 1965 to January 1973. And I would always be proud of the primary school I went to, regardless of the fact that I was not selected to join secondary school from there.

CHAPTER 6

NO LONGER NAÏVE

Seven years had passed since I left Tukuyu. Many things had changed by the time I went back in January 1973. They were not the way I left them. The *salala* was no longer there. People collected water in buckets to their homes. Small huts used as bathrooms had been constructed at each home. The traditional water management systems seemed less functional. The elders who used to command a lot of respect seemed to have lost some of their powers. They could no longer influence the course of things.

Farmers in the village were planting cabbage and sugarcane on the stream's banks. Some had also dug fishponds. One afternoon I went to our pond to fish with my cousin. My cousin showed me how to put bait on a hook. The bait was a worm we had found in the soil near the pond. After trying several times I caught a fish. Dusk was slowly encroached the day. We left for home. "This must have been the biggest fish in the pond," my father shouted.

But so much water had been diverted to the ponds. Lina stream that provided water for the *salala*, was almost dry. I visited the rock where we used to lie and bask in the sun after taking bath. Only a small portion of it remained bare. The other half was covered by eroded soil.

I asked my old friends to take me to the guava forest. They just laughed because the place didn't have a single guava tree left. The forest had been cleared for an *umoja* farm. Many other lands where I used to see guava trees had been cleared for biannual crops. Indeed, the virgin soil had been upturned. Unfortunately, the clearance didn't consider medicinal plants. For example, when I asked my mama about a piece of *pupwe* root, she laughed ironically and commented: "Yes, would you find *pupwe* today? That is a thing of the past." She concluded. The same applied to the veterinary medicines like *iloboka*; they were hardly found. When a cow was sick a farmer had to report to a veterinary doctor at *Bomani*.

The villagers' involvement in collective farm activities was part of the implementation of the post Arusha Declaration economic system. I saw the piece of land when it was virgin. I thought the acreage of the land was just too small to make any significant contribution to the common basket.

The *Umoja* farm and other collective projects were being supervised by the village administration. Immediate supervision had been delegated to respective committees. My father was appointed by the village authority to lead the Defense and Security Committee. I found the appointment a bit ironical; a church elder for defense and security? I didn't doubt my father's capabilities and commitment for that position but I doubted whether he clearly knew his mandate in that capacity.

However, the influence of TANU, the ruling party then, was quite obvious even at the village level. It was, for instance, not uncommon to hear people teasing each other: "*Songela TANU ngali ngukomile lijolo,*" which literally meant: "You should be thankful to TANU, had it not been that the party had established the rule of law, I could have beaten you a long time ago."

Mount Rungwe still looked like a royal guard on his sentry. It was well positioned like a custodian to the naivety. That notwithstanding, the naivety of the 1960s had gone.

The owner of the village *pombe* shop had died and the business had collapsed. The closure of the *pombe* shop meant that the village received few strangers. Some people who used to visit our village often for a drink were no longer seen in the village. The man who parked his Railegh bicycle at our home, the man who never parted with his donkey and the superman were no longer seen in the village. The end of the *pombe* shop was the end of seeing them.

Poll tax had been abolished so the fear for tax collectors was no longer there.

I could go to Tukuyu town without asking for permission from my parents. But my friends and I made sure that we returned to the village before sunset. We still feared *pabusisya*. The place had not changed. Even adults did not boast of passing this place with ease after night fall.

At the town centre, Indian shops were not as many as they used to be. Some owners had left for Mbeya and other bigger towns. I was told that what used to be the biggest shop in town run by an Indian trader had been closed. But in the same building a Public Trading Company had opened a wholesale shop. In the streets new trading actors had emerged. These were cooperative shops. The same applied to our village, a cooperative shop had been established. I could reckon the old system under which private traders like Samiso used to operate was simply incompatible to the new economic system.

The number of Indian shopkeepers had dwindled a lot. Many of the commercial buildings that were once owned by Indian traders had dilapidated and badly needed huge repairs as well as fresh painting. Coincidentally, in one of those rainy days, an ill wind ripped off the roof of one of the temples. Sadly, there was no one to rehabilitate it. The situation was just like that, people saw the damage that had been impacted on the temple by the wind but nobody seemed interested to do something. The damaged temple looked lonely and vulnerable. With the rainy climate in that part of the country, and due to lack of care, it did not take long before the temple eventually collapsed.

Behind the counters of some of the shops where I used to see Indian shopkeepers there were Bene's kinsmen. The Waswahili traders were still there but as a community they were not as distinct as they used to be. One of the reasons could be that the number of Kiswahili speakers had increased. Thus, it was as if everyone had become a Mswahili. It was with much difficult that one could identify the original Waswahili.

Our family had a special economic relationship with Samiso. He was an Indian trader who had agreed with my father for the supply of milk. He sold male clothes and school uniforms. My father paid his bill at the end of the month. Sometimes my father would borrow a shirt from the shop and ask Samiso to deduct from the milk money. When Samiso departed, the family no longer had a reliable buyer of milk.

Thus, Samiso's departure reduced the family's access to clothes. Then, more and more Indian traders departed and more and more shops closed. Inwardly, I felt sorry for my home town. I thought the traders gave a certain flavour to my town. The status of the town seemed higher with the presence of the traders. Without the traders I saw a hollow town. Their departure affected the tailors and many other families. Moreover, the decline of coffee, as a cash crop, compounded the economic challenges at the household level.

My father's economic activities were affected too. Some coffee trees were dead. Others looked too old to bear any berries. In the neighbourhood some farmers had abandoned coffee altogether. They planted tea in their farms to replace coffee. The price of coffee was not as attractive as it used to be.

I gathered that the tea buyers did not pay more than what the coffee buyers paid. The difference, however, was that tea leaves could be picked thrice a week. The farmers carried the leaves to a nearby buying station where they would be given a voucher. At the end of the same month that they sold the tea they got paid. Farmers seemed to have been excited by this arrangement. They preferred earning money every month like government employees.

My father neither shifted to tea growing nor paid much attention on the remaining coffee trees. He had bought three cows and he paid more attention to them than to the cash crop. Gradually, coffee trees were dying, one by one until they could hardly be seen on our farm. The cooperative society was not active as it used to be those days. The society still had offices there, but one could hardly see the life and confidence it used to radiate. She looked like breathing her last air!

The three cows had names according to their natural looks. The brownish one was called fumbe, the stripped one (like a zebra) was called sulula and the one without horns was called puli. Puli gave more milk than fumbe and sulula and she was very meek and docile. It was not a problem to milk her. Fumbe gave a little milk and she was very stubborn. It was not possible to milk her without tying her legs. Even that did not completely stop her from kicking. Sometimes she kicked the container with the very milk from her. Sulula was moderate, not harsh but not meek.

The cows could not be taken out to graze because the population had increased and most of the former grazing fields had been cultivated. My father tasked me with feeding the cows on Saturdays, Sundays and school holidays. I had to fetch grass and fill the manger in the cow shed. "You didn't give the cows enough grass', my father shouted. "But I did fill the manger twice," I replied. "But can't you see that their bellies are sunken," he said pointing at the sunken part of the belly. From that day I learned to tell if the cows had eaten enough grass. I found that I had to feed them twice in a day and take them out to a water trough on the ground in from of our home. They bounded as they approached the trough. I further learned that the cows bounded when they had enough fodder.

The other change at our home was that my father had almost finished the construction of another house. It contained a sitting room and three bedrooms. But he made the bricks himself because Bene, the man who made the bricks for the other house, had left. But people of his tribe could still be seen around. Some had permanently settled in the area. They mostly involved themselves in business. Several buses and shops could be identified with them. Some youths from our village worked for them.

Nevertheless, I appreciated the role played by the Waswahili community. Consciously or unconsciously, they played the role of custodianship. They protected the language and did not surrender to the pressure of the local language. Had they surrendered, the Kiswahili language would have survived.

But those Ladies and Gentlemen behind the selling counters of the companies used Kiswahili. I saw some of them at the Cathedral in town. They donned shirt and tie and nice coats with expensive pens hung on their pockets. I got the impression that they were learned people and they were not supposed to speak Kinyakyusa, especially in places of work. The church service at the Cathedral was conducted in Kiswahili except when the priest wanted to stress a point, he used Kinyakyusa. It was that kind of new development on the economic and social fronts that put pressure on the people to learn Kiswahili.

While the changes that compelled people to learn Kiswahili were taking place, the government established an adult education class in our village. Interestingly, the teacher who taught me at the bush school was the one teaching the adult education class. My mother joined the class where she learned Kiswahili. And after some lessons she could speak it, though not fluently. And for the first time she could read and write her name.

She could then read her Bible and the hymn book, though they were available versions in Kinyakyusa, she had not been able to read them. From her class she didn't have many books but they kind of triggered the need of having a book shelf in our home.

"You have to make a book shelf," my father rather ordered one evening. He showed me a piece of wood, a handful of nails and a saw. "If you fail everyone here will laugh at you," he said with a light tone, as I measured the wood. My mother, my brother and his friends were around. I felt a bit cold in my stomach. I panicked a bit but I quickly gained courage. I recalled what I learned in my carpentry class in Precious Stone Town: I sawed the wood into a number of pieces and nailed them to make a book shelf. In about an hour I was through. It was a simple shelf but I was proud of it. I handed it to my father with a smile. He took it into the living room. Most of the books on the shelf were church books but somehow, *Great Ponds*, a novel by Elechi Amadi, was also there. My brother, who was in secondary school by then, must have brought it. Later I read it as my first English novel.

CHAPTER 7

PASSED VERSUS SELECTED

In 1974 I got a chance to repeat Standard VII at Tukuyu. I assessed myself and recalled that I was weak in English and Mathematics. I decided to look for text books of those subjects, apart from those we had in class. One book: *"Mwandani wa Mwanafunzi,"* The student Companion, published in Kenya, proved to be a very good book for me. I spent many hours in my room doing the given questions and checking for the answers provided.

A day would not end without doing English and Mathematics exercises. In the subjects tests that we did in the class I always scored the highest marks. Our mathematics teacher used to ask me to demonstrate on how to solve a problem on the black board. I would do it so quickly and give the correct answer. My fellow students branded the methods I applied as "Fellowes' Method".

The day I especially remember is when a manager of a bank branch came to our school. He talked about the banking business and the interest that the bank gave to its client. He explained how the interest was calculated. "Can anyone show us on the black board how to calculate the interest basing on what I have explained," he asked. I walked to the front and put the calculation on the blackboard. "He knows mathematics, *hesabu zimo*," I heard him saying as I was getting to the answer. When I finished he and the class clapped for me, I had it correct.

Back home I told my mother about the visit of the men from the Bank. I further told her that I would like to open a bank account. "May I have five shillings for opening a bank account," I asked her. She smiled. From the smile I could tell that she would give me the money. I was right. In a while she untied a knot on her khanga. I looked on as the knot where she had secured several coins opened like a purse. She picked a five shillings coin and gave me.

The following morning I went to the Bank. I walked inside the Bank. It was crowded. Nobody seemed to notice my presence. And I could see that I was the only one from my school who was there that morning. Behind the counter men in white shirts and tie looked busy with papers and pens. "Would I be able to open an account? Where do I start? What would I tell my mother? Am I going to tell her that I could not make it?" I asked myself. I felt my heart thumping. Standing behind the counter, not knowing what to do, I saw the Bank Manager walking down the staircase. I walked towards him. "How are you," he greeted me with a broad smile. "I am fine. I have come to open an account," I said. He called one of the staff behind the counter. I recognized him; he was with the branch manager during the visit to our school. "Help this boy to open an account," the manager told the staff. He then disappeared behind the people who stood in a zigzagged queue.

The staff, assisting me, did most of the writing on the forms while I looked on. In a while I walked out of the bank with a red passbook in my hand. It indicated a balance of five shillings. I felt that I was clever. And it was as if everybody I met on the street could see that. At home we agreed with my mother that she would be giving me five shillings every month to deposit into my bank account.

I was in town when news spread around that the standard seven results had been posted at the district education office. A bit nervous, I walked to the place. There were a few boys and girls looking at the notice board. Those standing close the board had their index fingers moving on a list of names. I was about two metres from the board. I saw my name, though it was wrongly spelt. Instead of Fellowes Ambilikile Mwaisela it was written "Fellow Ambilile" But I was sure that it was me because at my school there was no one with a name similar to mine. I looked over the list once again. There was no other name from my school. Out of about forty pupils, so it meant, I was the only one selected to join a secondary school. I had passed. I wished those people in Precious Stone Town had known that I had passed. I was no longer among those whom they said have "failed".

I didn't feel the ground as I walked to the central market place where my father had started a small business of selling fish. I told him: "I have passed." I asked him for a Coca Cola drink. He gave me money to buy the drink. "You have to think of rewarding me," I said as I sat drinking the Coca Cola. "You are not the first one to be selected to join a secondary school," he replied. I had not expected such a reply. I had expected him to see me as someone who had "passed" and not simply "selected".

Then I told him about my name not being correctly written. "It is a just a mistake by those clerks," he replied and turned to listen to a buyer. I gulped the drink, bade him a good afternoon and left for home.

On the way home I assessed myself and thought that I was more important to my family, after the results, than before. In the evening my father seemed to be readily available to chat with me than any time before. We talked many things that were to come: the joining instructions and things that I would have to buy. As everything seemed fine my brother, Daniel, said: "But I will have to ask Ntuli to protect you from the bullying of form twos." "Who is Ntuli?" my father asked. "He is one of my friends. He is a form three student at Levavi Oculos, where Fellowes is going. In January next year, when Fellowes will be in form one he will be in form four," Daniel added. With what my brother said I felt relieved from the fear of bullies.

CHAPTER 8

HUMBLE LIKE A CHAMELEON

We who had been selected to join Form One at Levavi Oculos in 1975 had to report at the school earlier than the rest. In the joining letter it was also stated that I should take with me a hand hoe because the school not only taught Agricultural Science in the classroom but also had gardens for the students to attend. My brother, Daniel, was to escort me to the school. By then he had completed Form Four at Tabora Boys' Secondary School. My father and I believed that he had enough travel experience to take me to the school in Mbeya.

Before escorting me there he introduced me to his friend Ntuli. He was short and slender. His right hand was somewhat disabled. Daniel especially asked him to protect me from Form Two bullies. "How would Ntuli protect me?" I asked Daniel as we walked to the bus station. He didn't respond as quickly as I expected. "He doesn't seem to be strong enough," I said loudly. "But he is in Form Four," Daniel replied.

Daniel escorted me up to Mbeya then up to the school dormitory. He then left for Tukuyu by the last evening bus. I got acquainted with Ali and Sammy. They were joining Form One as well. We were curious to know more about the school environment. We strolled around other dormitories, the dining hall, the classrooms, the play grounds and the assembly hall. The words "Don't scramble" caught our eyes for they were on every wall. None of us knew what the "slogan" meant. It was, however, clear that it was a warning note to Form One students.

I was particularly surprised because it was our first time to be at the school. "Why should somebody make such anticipation against us?" I could kind of hear the tone of the writer or writers. It was harsh and not welcoming. These words were contrary to what the school logo seemed to communicate.

The logo was painted on the front wall of the assembly hall. It included the portrait of a chameleon stepping on a red flower with its eyes solemnly looking upward. The motto on the logo was "*LEVAVI OCULOS*" many, if not all of us, did not know what the words meant.

Some students said the language in which the motto was written was Latin but nobody seemed to be sure. One day, I happened to be among the students assigned to polish the floor of the assembly hall that was made of woodblocks from teak tree. The school was expecting a dignitary from town. Then the second master came to check how we were proceeding with the task. We took trouble to ask him the meaning of *Levavi Oculos*. "Let us be humble like a chameleon," he explained.

The school was situated on a relatively higher ground facing a mountain. On the north it bordered a river and on the south it bordered a dairy farm. Across the river there was a coffee farm. The farm was at the foot of the mountain. It was said that the coffee farm and the dairy farms used to belong to a white settler.

The dairy farm was still owned by the farmer while the coffee farm had been turned into a state property. The dairy farm had a fascinating scenery: acacia trees, Friesian cows eating grass, and a white mansion beside the river. The mansion faced the mountain as well. It had a garden with jacaranda trees, swings for children and a hammock. A white girl was swinging on the hammock when my friend and I passed by. The purple flowers of the jacaranda added to the beauty of the scenery.

There were stories around that at one time there were many white people in the area than at the time when I joined the school. It was even said that the school used to be for kids of rich white farmers and that the pupils came from as far as the former North Rhodesia, which later became Zambia.

The history of the school, so it was said, could be traced to about five decades. The buildings and a vehicle scrap in front of the carpentry shop could testify to that. Since the school did not plan an orientation for new comers, rumour mongers filled the gap. And the problem was, of course, how to get the truth. Truth and false statements could not be differentiated.

Our time as new comers was not easy. The senior students who were expected to be as humble as a chameleon had their own way of giving the orientation. They planned the orientation with a stereotyped picture of a Form One student impressed in their minds.

To them a Form One student (*Bazoka*) was a son of a peasant from the bush (*mshamba*) who confused a flush toilet for a laundry machine. According to the *juaji* (bullies) a typical Form One could not withstand normal boarding school problems. He would write several letters home to ask for pocket money. When he thought his parents might be fed up with his requests he would invent lies. The common cliché was that a Form One student would write a letter to his father telling him that he had broken an *amoeba* and that the headmaster wanted him to pay immediately or face a summary dismissal. And the stereotyped father of a Form One boy was supposed to be a panicky, illiterate peasant who upon receipt of the letter would send the money *pronto*.

Thus, the *juaji* demanded money from Form One students directly or indirectly. For example, one would be given twenty cents and asked to buy a packet of cigarette and return change to the sender. But in reality the poor Form One student would have to pay from his own pocket because a packet of cigarette was sold at around four shillings. I considered myself lucky. Ntuli came to our dormitory and announced to the Form Two students: "This is my *bazoka*. Try to bother him and I will deal with you individually," he said in a heavy voice with his hand rested on my shoulder. I didn't like when he said "my *bazoka*" but in that context it assured my protection and I had to accept it, anyway. About a week passed after Ntuli had declared me as his *bazoka*, a bunch of drunken form twos came to our dormitory. I saw them moving along the row of beds where the form ones slept. They removed their blankets leaving them uncovered. I waited to see what would happen to me. One of them came closer. I became a bit sweaty. "Leave that one he is Ntuli's *bazoka*," another one ordered.

Not every *juaji* was a bully but generally the students in the upper forms were very influential. They impacted certain habits onto Form One students. Some of my dormitory mates became smokers. I became a smoker too. But I would pray that my parents should not know.

The hidden social life of the school could destroy one's moral standard. But there was a lot of destruction as well on the school infrastructure. Not much care, for instance, was taken to the facilities that used to function normally under the former management: The gymnasium, the swimming pool and the laundry machine.

The gymnasium had an indoor basketball pitch. The floor of the pitch was made of wood. We did not, however, see much of the indoor pitch because the school received a lot of fertilizer bags for the farm. The bags were stored there as the school did not have a warehouse. The wooden floor collapsed because it could not withstand the weight of the fertilizer bags. And that was the end of it.

The school glass windows and water heating systems had been broken during the school's biggest riot in its history. It was said that the riot happened when the school was turned into a public one. Before the school turned public and admitted students from the peasantry, the school was a private one.

According to the school tradition, it all started when those students who used to pay fees questioned: "Why should the newcomers, of the year the school turned public, enjoy the nice facilities of the school for free?" They claimed that the nice facilities of the school were a result of the fees they paid. Thus they would not let someone who had not paid any money to have a secure admission to the school and enjoy the facilities. The riot broke out and the school was left devastated.

Apparently the school had two distinctive eras: before it turned public and after it became a public school. The pre-public era saw to it that the students got a treatment that deserved the fees their parents paid. The students' dormitories had water heaters in the bathrooms. There were attendants to take care of the beddings. There were gardeners to cut grass and trim the hedges. There was a laundry machine and an attendant in that respect. The cleanliness of the classroom and the dormitories was taken care of by the cleaners. So the students were there just to study.

Then came the post private era, when things changed. The students had to take cold water because the school could not afford such a luxury with its limited budget for electricity. The budget was limited for other items too. Thus, it followed that the students had to take care of their personal hygiene as well as the cleanliness of the environment. For that reason the laundry unit was closed. Most remarkably the students had to participate in producing food for their own consumption. The school had about twenty acres of land. In order to produce enough maize to feed the population of a thousand students, the school had to apply fertilizer. It was for this purpose that the fertilizer bags that destroyed the gymnasium floor were brought to the school.

The students were involved in other farm activities. The activities were commonly known as agricultural projects. The projects included the maize farm, a poultry unit, a small dairy unit with about five cows and horticulture. As it was at Precious Stone Town primary School, even here Education for Self-Reliance meant working in the *shamba*. But here the *shamba* work also acted as practical lessons. For example, we learned how to apply pesticides and chemical fertilizers. We were trained to make seed beds and transplant seedlings.

I didn't know how much came from the agricultural projects. But I knew that there was some pilferage. Students stole maize from the farm and roasted or cooked it using homemade heaters. Tomatoes and onions from the garden were picked and students made stew. Eggs were also stolen from the poultry unit. Despite the pilferage a lot of what we produced in the maize farm and horticultural garden reached the cafeteria. Most of the *shamba* work, cleanliness of classrooms and dormitories and order in the mess was supervised by prefects and monitors. As a monitor I had to note the names of those who dodged *shamba* work and report to the class master. And they would be given more work or a tougher one than what they dodged.

I think the headmaster and his team succeeded to delegate authority to students. But the school's administrative machinery could not stop students from sneaking out. Some students even went to drinking places nearby. But some of us went to a movie hall a few kilometres away. The movies were shown by the Chinese who were by then constructing a railway line from Dar- es-Salaam to Kapiri Mposhi in Zambia.

The railway was named *Uhuru* (Independence) Railway. The construction of the railway followed the decision of the ruler of South Rhodesia to close the border with Zambia. The action denied Zambia access to South African ports.

They were movies about wars. It was clear that the movies showed the Chinese army fighting the enemy troops. The movies showed very brave Chinese soldiers. Their army always emerged victorious. I liked the movies. Many students liked the movies too. We identified ourselves with the Chinese soldiers. To us the Chinese soldiers, as characters in the movies, were heroes because they fought the oppressor.

The concept of oppression was not new to us. One of our teachers was a South African. On 21st March of every year, he led us on the commemoration of those who were massacred at Sharpeville. A total of 69 people died when police opened fire to a group that held a peaceful protest against carrying pass books on 21st March 1960 around Sharpeville police station. Carrying of pass books was enforceable by the Pass Law. The law was one of the instruments of the Apartheid system. On that occasion Comrade XAmandla, our teacher from South Africa, would be given a chance to address the school assembly.

Comrade XAmandla, a handsome man, with a stout physique, maintained a clean shave. He had a heavy voice. It was common to see him with his pipe. Students especially knew him for his good heartedness. He did not identify himself with any freedom fighters movement, but he condemned the Apartheid system. Whenever he was given the chance to speak he would begin with the words "They oppress us because of our inferiority". As he was speaking the students maintained deep silence. Then, the Headmaster would ask Bryson, another teacher, to translate. Bryson would say in Kiswahili; "*Wanatuonea sisi wanyonge*".

Comrade XAmandla's speeches increased my interest in South African protest literature. I read *The Party* by James Matthews, *Quartet* by Richard Rive, *Mine Boy* and *A Wrath for Udomo* by Peter Abrahams, and *Inside Boss* by David Winter. But above all I found the book: *Traitor of my Heart*, by Rian Malan as the most interesting and depicting the true picture of South Africa. The readings increased my understanding about Apartheid. I also learned that according to the system Comrade XAmandla was classified as a coloured.

Though we liked the Chinese movies, from which we learned more about oppression, it needed extra courage to sneak out of the school. The teacher on duty would make a surprise roll call. Those not present would, on the following day, be punished. One of the punishments most hated was to clean the dormitory toilets.

The toilets were not a place to go. The school provided toilet papers but many students would soon run out of one before being provided with another. It was surprising that some would use maize cobs instead of a toilet paper. The maize cobs blocked the passage of the excreta. But the users of the facility ignored this fact. They continued to deposit the excreta until the whole basin was full. Then there would be the spill over. The excreta spread on the floor. The punishment would last a week or more depending on how the prefect rated the offender. But even this punishment could not deter some of us from going to the movies. The movies continued to be an irresistible attraction.

Throughout the week our lunch consisted of *ugali* served with beans while supper consisted of rice served with beans except on Sundays when we had rice served with beef. Taking a rice and beef meal in the dining hall was easier said than done. When

it was several minutes to the dining time
the students of upper classes would walk
to the dining hall. They would be hovering
around the dining hall like scavengers. They
would be observing every movement of the
cook on duty. The cook on duty was the one
supposed to ring a bell to allow people in.
But not on the day when there was rice and
beef; nobody was patient enough to wait
for the bell to ring. They would be looking
at the hand of the cook that held the bell.
Movements of other body parts of the cook
did not matter, what mattered was the hand
that held the bell.

The students crushed inside and dived
on to the tables with food dishes. One day it
was even worse for me and a few other form
one students. Some *juaji* took all the food
from our table. I looked for Ntuli and told
him of what happened. He took me to the
head prefect. "How many of you did not get
food from your table," he asked me. "Four
of us," I replied. He sent another prefect to
look for the boys and then he took the five
of us to the chief cook. The chief cook,
nicknamed "Bob" was a short person with
protruded biceps. Students were afraid of
him for it was said some years back he beat a

juaji who tried to take food from the kitchen. We stood far from Bob as the head prefect talked with him. "There is no food left except some milk and oranges in the cold room," the head prefect told us after talking with Bob. Each of us got a litre of cold milk and two oranges for supper. I drunk the milk then ate the oranges. For about three days I had a stomach upset. And I was kind of feeling feverish.

Another aspect of school life was that of reading novels. It was actually more than a hobby. It was a sub-culture within the school culture. I was very comfortable with this sub-culture. Those of us who "subscribed" to this sub-culture came to know one another. We established an informal club of novel readers.

I developed the habit of reading. My favourite titles and other members of the club were novels written by James Hadley Chase. These were mainly crime or detective novels. They were published by either Panther or Corge. The ones published by Panther were printed in smaller fonts of ten points while Corge publications were done on twelve point fonts. Thus while a Panther book would have around one hundred and fifty pages a Corge publication would be about two hundred pages long.

All in all, I was able to finish a novel in a day and narrate the story to my mates. Actually it was one of the rules of the "club" that once you borrow a novel you have to finish in a day so that you will pass it to another member. The reading was mostly done on Saturdays and Sundays. With this timetable I could list more than sixty titles of James Hadley Chase that I read between Form Two and Four. A fiction by Robert Louis Stevenson, *The Treasure Island*, was also among the favourites. The Kiswahili version: *Kisiwa Chenye Hazina*, was more in circulation than the English one. Many students who read the book, including myself, were captivated by the characterisation of Long John Silver or John Fedha, as he was called in the Kiswahili version. Apart from reading fiction, I also read some other titles that were non-fiction. These included *Valachi Papers*, *Papilon*, *Branco*, and a few titles on psychology: *Love Without Fear* and *Who Do You think You Are?*

The latter book helped me to learn more about myself, to borrow the words of the author, "just as a pebble on the beach". The book also taught me to understand human beings as actors. The author repeatedly argued that "we are all actors". Thus sometimes I don't talk to or take people seriously because I know there is that element of acting in almost all human beings. He or she can act depending on what and where he or she is.

In those days there were also small volumes strictly circulated among members of the readers' club. They included: *One by One*, *After Four Thirty*, *My Dear Bottle* and *Fit for Human Consumption*. These books were later banned. I suspect the reason behind was that they were pornographic. I cannot dispute this reason but I think the books had some good lessons. I read them positively. They increased my understanding on the relationship between a man and a woman. Later when I came to live at Ohio and Garden streets in Dar es Salaam, I saw with my naked eyes some of the things written in the banned books. I further understood of things around the world through the Geography class. Our teacher was an old Indian gentleman. We nicknamed him "Brahmaputra" because we were fascinated by the way he pronounced Brahmaputra River in India. He also taught us about

Ganges River in India and Yellow River in China. That was within the Form Two syllabus that covered India "sub continent" and China. Later in Form Three and Four, the syllabus included Ghana, Nigeria and South Africa.

Within the same period, between 1975 and 1978, the Uhuru Railway was opened and operated with limited passenger services trains. The nearby station at Iyunga was opened. The station became more exciting than the movies. Other students and I were particularly attracted by the Congolese music that was played through a cassette player for several hours.

The gentleman or lady who was in control of the cassette player soothed our hearts. He played our faourites: *Memi* by Orchestra Kiam, *Bitota* by Orchestra Fuka Fuka, *Sekizengi* by Orchestra Lipualipua. *Nsayi* and *Mangala* by Orchestra Veve. Rarely did she or he play the song *Salama* by Safari Trippers. I liked these songs. Many students enjoyed the music as well. Some, even abandoned classes and went to the station to listen to the music. Others danced before the waiting passengers at the station. The influence of the music played at the station was everlasting. At that time I could not imagine that twelve years later I would start building my own collection of Congolese music.

Before the experience at the station, I knew only four songs. *Mado* by TP OK Jazz, *Tambola na Mokili* by Orchestra Conga, *Maseke ya Meme* and *Matondo ya Beya* by Negro Success. In my opinion the Congolese music was at its best in the sixties to mid seventies.

Towards the end of 1978, our final year at school, Idi Amin troops of Uganda invaded Tanzania. The local English newspaper identified the invaded part as Kagera salient. I remembered my fine art teacher in Precious Stone Town. I wondered what he felt when our country was going to war with the country where he studied.

Mwalimu delivered a speech in which he stressed: "*Uwezo wa kumpiga tunao, sababu ya kumpiga tunayo na nia ya kumpiga tunayo*". Mwalimu added that our army was a defense force and by defense we meant it. In that context he stressed that our army was not an aggression force. After the speech almost every student recited the poetic speech. The students expressed their moral support and paid attention to every piece of information about the development of the war. There were two sources of information: the radio and the government newspapers.

Our country was engaged in the war at a time when we were just about to begin our final examinations. Never the less the examinations went on as planned and the four years of our secondary education came to an end. For the four years that I had been there I was a class monitor. During the graduation ceremony, class monitors and prefects were awarded with certificates of appreciation. I looked at my certificate. Below my name it stated: "Character- Good and Hard working". The words "good and hard working" were bolded in black ink.

That evening however, it was the song from Lumumba House that touched my heart. The house prefect was awarded a prize because of the song. It was about the liberation of Africa. I can remember part of it:

Hivi leo bara letu la Afrika uwanja mkubwa,
Wa mapambano makali sana,
ya kumtoa mkoloni,
Watanzania tuliamua,
Mwaka wa sabini na nne
Uwe mwaka wa ukombozi,
Afrika nzima ikombolewe.

Today our African continent is a field of
fierce battle,
    To oust the colonialists,
    We, Tanzanians, decided,
    That nineteen seventy four,
    Should be the year for liberation,
    The whole of Africa must be liberated.

The song reminded me of a man who
lived near Anna, one of my mother's younger
sisters. The man sometimes came to Anna's
home when I happened to be visiting her.
He told me that he was a freedom fighter
from Zimbabwe.

After the graduation ceremony, as
every other form four student did, I went
to the dormitory to pack my bag. I could
not feel that warmth of togetherness that
I used to feel before the graduation. The
social atmosphere changed, it became cold.
Everyone seemed to be a distance away
from everyone else. Even Ali seemed to be a
distance away from me, though he was next
to me packing his bag. Here was the day
we had been waiting for yet soon after the
ceremony it did not give me the happiness
I thought it would. One part of me was

eager to leave, but the other part longed for a continued stay with my friend.

The arrival of EAR&H buses, that the school administration had hired to take us to the main station in town, even made the situation worse for me. I nearly wept when it was time to say good bye to Ali, who was to take a different bus to a different route. Around 3.00 I boarded the bus. Students of lower forms crowded around the bus. They yelled as the bus drove out of the parking lot and moved towards Mbeya town. From Mbeya town took the road to Itigi. The travel was fine until around 8.00 pm when the bus broke down. It was deep in the heart of the Miombo forest. Tsetse flies were hovering all over the place. They landed on our bodies. They stung and sucked our blood and off they flew like enemy choppers. The' bombardment' continued nonstop. I had never been stung by a tsetse fly before. One had landed on left arm. I didn't feel it until it had sucked blood out of me. I smashed it with my right hand. It burst and blood spilled out of its stomach, more than what I had seen from a mosquito.

I had not carried something to eat with me. The breakdown happened at the early

hours of the night. In the afternoon of the
following day I felt hungry and dizzy. The
sun's heat was strong and tsetse flies were
a constant menace. I maintained silence
because talking would waste the little energy
that was still with me. If we had not had the
breakdown we would have reached Itigi at
around five in the morning.

Some men amongst passenger decided
to walk to Kambi Katoto to look for water
and food. A ten miles walk, in the sun and
with the unwanted company of tsetse flies.
A few of us, a school boy (that's me), two
girls from Loleza Secondary School, several
women and children and the driver stayed
behind. The driver did not show signs of
wearing down. He looked composed, stable
and patient. Despite the afternoon heat he
still had on him the khaki coat, the uniform
of the corporation. I saw the image of the
corporation in him. I admired his calmness.
We had been stranded in the middle of the
forest but that man did not seem to lose
courage.

The schoolgirls had carried sandwiches
with them and a bottle of concentrated
orange juice. In the afternoon the girls
diluted the juice. They offered half a cup of

the drink and a piece of bread to the driver. They did the same to me. I took the bread and the juice in seconds. I felt life coming back to me.

At about sunset the men who went to Kambi Katoto returned with water and food. They sat under the tree shades to drink and eat with those who accompanied them.

At around 10.00 pm another bus came to take us. Our driver told us to get on board of the other bus. He remained behind with the two mechanics, brought by the other bus. I felt sorry for him as our bus drove off. He seemed to me just too innocent to run into such a difficulty.

Our bus arrived in time for a train connection at Itigi. I disembarked from the train at Shinyanga at 12.00pm. The night was very cold. I knew of a place where they sold ginger tea. It was within the station area. I went there. The tea seller, a man with long white beard, was busy serving cups of tea to people surrounding him. I asked for a cup of tea. I sipped it with my lips feeling the heat of the cup. I felt a bit warm while sipping, but I felt cold soon after emptying the cup. I asked for another one. The cold wind persisted. "Take this khanga and cover yourself it is too cold," a woman next to me said. "No it is okay," I replied while shivering. "However cold it should be I wouldn't like to cover myself with a khanga," I said to myself. The night seemed too long. Before that experience I thought Tukuyu had the coldest nights.

When the day was just breaking, I boarded a bus to Precious Stone Town. It was about a twenty kilometres drive on a dusty and bumpy road. I arrived at the town's gate before 8.00am. My uncle was there to meet me. After a week or so my uncle told me that there were temporary jobs with the GPMCL Company and that I should apply.

CHAPTER 9

YOUNG ADULTS AND ADULTS ALIKE

I received an acceptance letter, in about three week time since I sent the application, and advised to appear for interview at the big man's office. It was in February 1979. My application contained my academic and the appreciation certificates I was awarded at Levavi Oculos. The big man had a chain of supervisors below him: senior foreman, assistant senior foreman, foreman, assistant foreman, charge hand and a technician.

The interview lasted for hardly five minutes. While sitting on his chair he, showed me the map of the plant. Frankly speaking, I did not understand a thing. Then the interview continued.

"Did you pass Mathematics?"

"Yes I did."

"Which grade did you get?"

"I got a di (D)."

(Smiling) "You don't pass with a diii. Do you?"

The man did not refer to the appreciation certificate where my headmaster at Levavi Oculos defined me as a "good and hard working boy". And the interview was over. He summoned the engineer and asked him to take me to one of the head of departments. We drove in a Morris Minor pickup. I was handed over to an assistant senior foreman of fitting and turning workshop. I became part of the loyal workforce under him. The workforce included both men older than me and those younger than me. The younger ones had finished Standard VII and went to a two year course at the technical school. They were on apprenticeship arrangement whereby they were to be with the workshop for three years before having their employments confirmed.

I was within the mine plant area, the place, which as a child I could only see from a veranda in *Changanyiko*. Entrance to the area was strictly not allowed unless by special permission. The pass which one could use at the main gate was not acceptable for the purpose of entering the mine plant area. So for the seven years that I was there as a primary school pupil I never had the pass to visit the area. As soon as I entered the area, I felt like my status had been elevated. "I was a worker".

One of my first assignments was to make holes on an iron bar called channel, in the technical language. The technician made the measurement and punched marks on spots where he wanted the holes made. The drill which we used to make holes was driven by a motor. I was told that the channel was made of mild steel while the drill was high-speed steel.

I learned other things like different sizes of nuts and bolts: half inch, five eighth, and three quarter. I learned that some machines had nipples, again this was a technical language, and it was through them that grease could be pumped into the machine.

The workshop was built with channels, angles and iron sheets. Which meant it could be dismantled and reconstructed on another site. It had cranes fixed inside. The cranes were used for lifting heavy things like motors. I learned that many things had eyebolts fixed to them. It was through the eyebolt that they could be hooked and lifted. I learned that cranes had different capacities. The one in the workshop had a five ton capacity.

The workshop had its social aspect. One of the important social events was taking tea together at 10.00 every morning. Tea was self service. But it was the duty of Mzee Ichai Jipile to fill the electric kettle with water and switch it on. But one day there was no power so water did not boil.

At ten tools were put down and everyone was there ready for the tea. People stood there, arms akimbo, when they learned that there was no boiled water. No talking. Then suddenly the lights in the shop went on. A gesture that the electric power cut was over. I heard people (adults and young adults) shouting *Oyee!* Some high jumped. I never thought that both the adults and young adults would shout like that just for a cup of tea.

The plant was serviced every Thursday. On such a day we were posted to various sections of the plant. Thursday was the only day one could touch the sand containing the precious stones. The sand was there on the conveyor belts. I looked hard expecting to see a precious stone but I never saw one even once.

Not far from the workshop there was a place called pits. This was where heavy earth moving equipment the D6s and D8s and Draglines worked like the zealous rhinos and elephants in George Orwell's *Animal Farm*. Heavy duty trucks shuttled endlessly between the pits and the crushers. At the pits they were filled with the stony sand and at the crushers they emptied themselves. The children in *Changanyiko* called the trucks *manyunguleti* (plural) and *Nyunguleti* (singular). Equally busy were the operators of the machine that scooped the sand and loaded it onto the trucks. The children never fell short of names for anything. They christened the machine *kikomba maandazi* or simply *kikomba*.

Like many other words spoken by children in *Changanyiko* the origin of the word *nyunguleti* was not known. The *manyunguleti* worked like termites to and from the pits. They loaded and unloaded the precious sand all day long, all night long. The engines were only briefly switched off when drivers changed shifts.

The processing of the sand bearing precious stones would start in the pits, where the material was dug. Then the material would be carried by *Manyunguleti*. Those heavy duty trucks would unload the sand into the bins. Below the bins there were conveyor belts that would carry the material into the crusher where it would be crushed into fine sand. Another system of conveyor belts would carry the fine sand to the Central Processing Unit (CPU) of the plant. The final destination would be the sorting house.

The extraction of sand from the pits involved heavy machinery. Processing in the CPU involved heavy machinery too but ultimately the sorting house involved a man with a very light equipment - a man at the sorting house used a forceps like instrument to separate stones with higher value from those with low value. So in the end it was what came out of the sorting house that mattered.

When I looked at the plant system as a whole I got the imagination of a gigantic animal. The pits were its plate of food, the earth moving equipment its hands, the crushers its teeth, the conveyor belt it's esophagus, the CPU its stomach and the sorting house its small intestine; absorbing only the useful nutrients.

There were so many *manyunguleti*. They shuttled day and night between the pits and the bins. "When do you think the precious stones would be exhausted from the ground?" I asked my foreman. "They will not be exhausted any time soon. At least this generation will pass without seeing their exhaustion. You know there is something mystical about these stones. I can say the Precious Stone Town is forever," he remarked.

CHAPTER 10

THE POWER OF PROMISES

The days of temporary employment with the GPMCL were over. After my 'O' level education I was selected to join 'A' level at a school by the Great lake. I travelled to Mwanza where I was accommodated by an old friend. I stayed there for three days before I travelled by bus to the school. The journey took about seven hours. I heard that normally the journey would take six hours. But we took seven hours because we were delayed at a town halfway, by Speke gulf, before we reached our destination a traffic police officer stopped our bus. It had worn out tyres. The traffic police officer was not ready to let us go. Our driver disembarked from the bus. He was engaged in a dialogue with the officer. He pleaded with him that he should let the bus go. The officer insisted that he could not do so because the bus had such worn out tyres. *Angalia mwenyewe tairi vipara kabisa*. I heard some passengers complaining. "Why is he doing so? Doesn't he know that this is a public company bus?" The driver of the bus shared the same view. "This is a public bus *Bwana*. Allow us to continue with our safari. Where do we get money to buy new tyres?" He lamented. When more and more passengers complained, one passenger said: "The officer is right because he is adhering to professional ethics."

It was my first time to hear the words "professional ethics". I could only guess what they meant. I looked at the man. He was, probably in his early thirties. He looked educated and confident. I was impressed.

Eventually, the bus was released and we proceeded with our journey. We safely reached the town where the school was located in. I disembarked from the bus at the stand near the school. The school was located about two hundred metres off the highway. Thus, I carried my bag and walked towards the main entrance. I found some students who were kind enough to direct me to the headmaster's office for registration formalities. On one of the walls of the office, there was this famous quotation from the late Mwalimu J.K. Nyerere:

"Those who receive this privilege, therefore, have a duty to repay the sacrifice which others have made. They are like the man who has been given all the food available in a starving village in order that he might have the strength to bring supplies back from a distant place. If he takes this food and does not bring help to his brothers, he is a traitor. Similarly, if any one of the young men and women who are given an education by the people of this Republic adopt attitudes of superiority, or fail to use their knowledge to help the development of this country, then they are betraying our Union."

What particularly touched me was the simile: "They are like the man who has been given all the food available in a starving village in order that he might have the strength to bring supplies back from a distant place". This simile reminded me the story of Jacob's sons in the Bible, when they were sent by their father, from the famine-hit Canaan to go to buy food in Egypt (distant place). I imagined myself as being like one of those sons of Jacob sent to Egypt. How would my father Jacob feel if I had not brought back the food to Canaan? My heart pounded as I reflected on these wise words. I could not help thinking about my Uncle Ulimbakisya Ikumboka, who had been giving me pocket money ever since I started school.

I thought about my father and mother who also supported my education. They were making a lot of sacrifices to ensure that I receive adequate education to enable me become a productive member of my society. These words have remained with me, making me feel indebted to both my family and my country.

The school was located near the lake. Thanks to whoever had planned it to be where it was because we had a chronic water shortage and the lake water saved us. It was part of the school routine to put on duty some of the students to fetch water from the lake. The water was used for cooking. For personal hygiene, students were expected to go to the lake for washing clothes or taking bath.

Bathing at the lake did not follow rules like the ones in my home place. Here children and adults, young and old, women and men took bath almost in the same area. It was common to see an old man taking bath with someone qualified to be his grandchild. Women would be bathing a few metres away from men. Girls would be taking bath twenty metres from where boys were swimming. For some of us that looked like an orientation to a new culture. But I found it completely detestable.

The serious water shortage at the school also meant that the flush toilets in the dormitories could not function and they were dirty. The Headmaster was a humble person who, always seemed to be in a hurry. He had just graduated from the ruling party ideological college. He was still steaming with enthusiasm. He embarked on a campaign to maintain the cleanliness of the toilets regardless of the acute water shortage.

In the classroom I was exposed to another social setting. Most of my classmates engaged in all sorts of debate. It was as if the criterion for being selected to join the class was one's ability to debate. People would debate even on objective realities that did not need a debate at all. For example, one day someone entered the class and on the course of sitting down at his chair he said, "I saw Mdwanzi" (one of our teachers). The supposedly simple statement provoked a debate, which lasted for hours. Someone replied, "Did you see him or he saw you." Another one came with alterative statement: "You did not see him but you saw each other." In no time the entire class was involved in the debate. People took sides and each group defended its position.

But, there were some who were a bit exceptional. I remember, particularly, two of them. They were silent observers. They never actively participated in any of the informal debates. One day one of the 'philosophers' of the class was not at ease with the behaviour of the two, so he said: "Gentlemen, your silence either means you agree with all what we say or you judge all what we say as non-sense. Now tell us which is which?" Even that provocative statement did not get the silent observers involved in the debates. I admired those guys in many ways. For example, they never complained about food. Whether the food was good or bad they just ate it without complaining. While some of us would be eating and lamenting at the same time. They would eat silently. You could never tell the difference when they had money in their pocket or when they had none!

When it came to the food we ate at school most of us did not have an appetite. But this was not the case with the children from the surrounding community. Apparently the households where the children came from faced food shortages. Consecutive years of prolonged dry spells had scorched the farmers' crops. The children would be peeping through the holed bricks that made the dining hall. Hardly, had we left the dining hall than the children, literally, invaded the hall for whatever was left on the table. I had never seen something like that at Levavi Oculos.

Things were not all good with the school as well since even the school's ability to buy food was deteriorating. The Headmaster had announced that the school was getting less funds for food and other items in the budget. The quality of the food we ate deteriorated day after day. The rice we ate had a lot of sand and other particles. The beans we ate had been severely bored by bugs. The climax of the poor situation at the school was a month of eating food without a grain of salt. The students couldn't take it any longer. They boycotted the food. The school administration's response was to single out the so-called ring leaders and suspended them.

I found the decision of the school administration unreasonable. The boycott was actually a result of the leadership not talking with the students about the problem. The shortage of salt was well known. There was no salt in the entire region. The students were aware of that fact. Had the school administration communicated with them on that fact the students would have understood. I was sure if the message had been communicated in time the boycott could not have happened. The boycott was triggered by the failure to communicate the real situation at the right time.

Partly, I could attribute my point of view and the boycott to the influence of the readings that we studied in our Literature class. The readings were categorized into themes. One of the themes was Response of the Oppressed. Under this theme, for instance, we studied Sembene Ousmane's *God's Bits of Wood*, Bertolt Brecht's *The Caucasian Chalk Circle* and Ngugi wa Thiongo's *Petals of Blood*. Other key readers included: Chinua Achebe's *A Man of the People*, Henrik Ibsen's *An Enemy of the People*. These two last titles were highly satirical because the reader 'sees' who is the true 'man of the people' and who is the true 'enemy of the people'. In my own other readings, I read Charles Dickens' *Hard Times* and *Oliver Twist*. I was equally interested in regional geography. I remember, for instance, our teacher telling us about the railway line that extended from Moscow to Vladivostok, the port city on the extreme eastern part of Russia. According to our teacher the travel by train would take nine days. "Travelling for nine days within the same country?" Most of us in the class wondered.

Then came September 1980, eight months before the end of my Advanced Secondary education, coincidently, that was also the year for the General Elections. The school was divided between two camps. Teachers and students identified themselves with certain candidates. In that year's election, the parliamentary old guard was defending his seat against the newcomer. The division at the school level was serious. Anything one said anywhere mattered. People had no other perspective except the election campaign. Whatever one said would be linked with the campaign. I favoured the newcomer in that race.

The candidates who were contesting for the seat either themselves or their agents infiltrated the school community. They struggled to extend and strengthen their influence. The first to approach the community was the newcomer. I was there when he arrived and mingled himself with a small group of students. He introduced himself and boasted that he was a holder of a rare profession. He promised that given the opportunity to serve the people he would apply his profession to bring about development. He distributed pens to some students. A few days later he donated cooking oil. His agents made sure that every student knew who donated the stuff. The stuff was donated at a time when the school had such a limited budget that it could not afford to include cooking oil in the students' meal. So the stuff came at the right time.

On the other side, one of our teachers claimed that the old guard would assist his supporters to get chances to study abroad. A few days later the old guard himself came to the school and the teacher, who supported him, organized a meeting of students in the assembly hall. When it was time to speak, one of the men who accompanied the old guard delivered a speech. It was basically a list of things that he claimed had been

done by the old guard. Then there came a
list of promises. After the speech I raised
my hand. The students cheered. The teacher
who was moderating the meeting stood up
and said. "It is unfortunate that our visitor
has a tight schedule. He will not be able to
answer any question today. Please spare your
questions until next time." "Let Fellowes
ask the question," the students jeered. But
the teacher and the old guard stood up and
walked outside. The meeting was over. We
dispersed. I walked to the dormitory with a
difficult breathing, disappointed.

The students were also lured to attend
secret meetings at night. Some of us could
not attend our evening preparation classes.
My friend asked me to join the old guard's
camp. I declined. "The old guard had had
enough and we needed the newcomer for a
change," I told him.

I joined the newcomer's campaign team.
I attended one of the secret meetings at
night. The meeting took place inside the
house of an old man I knew to be an active
member of one of the local churches. We
were about twenty boys. We sat on the floor
squeezing one another. I didn't see any of
my close friends. But to my surprise the

following morning one of them told me where I was the previous night and all what we discussed in that meeting. I never again attended night meetings. But I also blamed myself for not joining the other group for I started believing in the promise of being sent abroad for studies. And for me captivating aspect of the promise was not the study but travelling abroad.

Those days there was a magazine that periodically circulated among the students. In one of its regular features was the KLM advertisement. It showed a plane landing at an airport in Amsterdam. The picture was colourful. I was filled with the desire to travel by the airline. Then I thought about the promise by the old guard: "the scholarship to study abroad". I thought I should think about my position. Should I maintain my position of not supporting the old guard?

I knew that if I offered to join the group they would readily accept me for I was particularly popular among the students for asking questions that would challenge what a politician had said. Fellow students branded "challenging questions" as "Fellowes" questions". Having realized this, sometimes the teacher moderating the meeting would suspect that I might raise a question that would not be answered satisfactorily. With such suspicion, he would skip me and give chances of asking questions to other students. In such cases the students would murmur. They would demand that I should be given the chance. Some teachers speculated that my questions might negatively affect the opinion of the candidate they favoured. They therefore arranged I should not be around on the day the candidates came to campaign at the school.

At the peak of the campaign in that year one of the teachers approached me and he succeeded in convincing me that I was a man of such brilliant ideas. I felt my head growing big. Then he told me that the finalists in the neighbouring school badly needed my input in a speech they were writing for their graduation day.

So I went to the school. I was given a warm welcome. I assisted in writing the speech. There were two guys from the host school, but only one made significant contributions. The other guy was just there. He had a fixed smile and agreed to whatever we suggested. He was very punctual to serve us with tea and food. He punctuated our conversation with jokes and laughter.

In the afternoon we had a comparatively nice lunch of rice and beef. A soft drink branded *Vimto* served as a dessert. The two guys escorted me to a certain distance before they left me to continue on my own. I was to cover a distance of seven kilometres on foot. I was not afraid of the distance. I felt big and important.

I arrived at school when the campaign was over. After supper I joined the debates that were doing a postmortem of the campaign meeting. I discovered that I was purposely exiled. I blamed myself for being such a fool for I should have discovered the trick.

The results of the election came out, the new comer had lost. I was disappointed. My friends who supported the old guard were happy, though I didn't see them going abroad for studies. The school days were over. In May 1981 we sat for our final examinations. The sessions took about two weeks. We boarded a ship and said goodbye to the Lake side town which had hosted us for two years. We sailed to Mwanza. During the journey I spent most of the time at the deck and gazed at the lake and at other times at the horizon. I remembered the story my friend Aziz told me a long time back. I thought I might as well see the chains descending from the sky to fish out the big snake that Aziz said it lived in the lake.

CHAPTER 11

BEYOND MY FATHER'S MEDICINE

While still with the GPMCL, I started
suffering from chest pains, sore throat
and breathing difficulties. It was a kind of
asthmatic condition. It was even worse when
I took tea with sugar or whenever I took
something sweet. I had to avoid tea with
sugar as well as sugary fruits like pawpaw.

I started searching for a cure by consulting
a number of doctors serially.
The first doctor to consult had many years
of experience. He worked for a public
hospital. When I entered the consultation
room I considered myself lucky to find
him on duty. I believed he would be able to
diagnose the problem. I explained to him
about my health condition. I was impressed
by his appearance. He was both a chubby
and muscular person. He looked bigger than
the consultation room. If one's health was
judged by appearance, then that man was

healthy. He probed me with his eyes from the moment I stepped in all the way until I got seated on the chair in front of him.

Using an expensive pen, he scribbled some notes as I was explaining. His stethoscope was hanging on his neck. Undoubtedly, the stethoscope showed not only that he was proud of being in the medical profession but also that he liked his job.

I took the card, on which he had written the prescription, to the pharmacist. The pharmacist read it and from a metal container, he scooped some drugs for me. He wrapped them in a piece of paper. He did it so skillfully like the Indian shopkeepers when they wrapped salt to customers during those memorable days in Tukuyu.

I was supposed to take one pill thrice a day. I took the drugs as per prescription. I finished the dose and there was no improvement at all. They did not work like *pupwe*, a small piece of a tree back that my father gave me for stomach ache when I was a child. That one worked a few minutes after I had chewed it.

After a month I decided to consult a second doctor. He was running a private dispensary in the major town near the

Precious Stone Town. On one of the walls of his dispensary he hung a billboard that indicated his name and his medical qualifications. On the billboard it read that he was an M.D. holder. The degree he obtained in one of the former communist countries in Eastern Europe.

Several minutes before I reached the dispensary I saw him on a bicycle. He was riding towards the dispensary. When I arrived he was already there. I entered into his consultation room.

I sat on the chair in front of his table. I faced him as I was explaining. He did not seem to be concentrating on what I was saying. His mind seemed to be wandering elsewhere. I did not see a stethoscope with him. Having listened or half listened to my explanation he told me that the problem I was suffering from was common among cotton ginnery workers. He injected me on an upper part of the arm. A few minutes after the injection I felt my body getting warmer. The muscles of my chest relaxed. I could breathe somewhat normally than before I received the injection.

The treatment put me in a better position as I was about to travel to Tukuyu. In May

1979 I was in Tukuyu. The relief didn't last long. The chest pain, the breathing difficulties and the sore throat all resumed to a level I could not bear any more without seeking for further medical assistance.

I decided to consult a third doctor. I went to a Private hospital within the district. While at the hospital I learned that they had a fast track option. I opted for the fast track. I paid the consultation fee and the nurse on duty led me to the doctor's room. I found a Black doctor. He wore a white overcoat. He did not talk with me but through his facial expression I knew that he was ready to hear my explanation. So I told him how I felt with my throat and chest. He did not say anything but prescribed some medications for me. After he had prescribed I could see that he immediately lost interest in me. He handed me the prescription sheet. As he had used his facial expression to let me explain my problem, in the same manner he indicated that I should find my way out. I proceeded to the pharmacy section to collect the medicine he had prescribed. From there I collected small white tablets. The tablets were of the size of a seed of sorghum. The dosage was one tablet per day for seven days. I finished the dosage but there was not a single bit of relief.

This was to be a fourth doctor I consulted. I returned to the same hospital. This time I met a White doctor. Upon seeing him I was hopeful. Unconsciously, I developed an assumption that the White doctor would be better than the Black one I found the other day.

I explained to him about my problem. I also explained about the medication I had taken before. He listened. Then he told me to stand up and face the widow and open my mouth. He said he would use the day light that came through the glass window instead of a torch. He pressed my tongue with a wooden instrument and looked down my throat.

In a short while he established that I had big tonsils. But he said that was normal as there were people with big tonsils and some with small tonsils. I was one of those with big tonsils and there was nothing wrong.

"But I suffer from a sore throat, chest discomfort and breathing difficulties," I complained.

"But you are not sick," he insisted.

"So what are you going to prescribe for

me?" I asked politely.

"I am not going to prescribe any medicine for you because you are not sick," he said rather impatiently.

I looked at him in a way that he should think about his opinion. But it was obvious that he wanted me to get out of the room. I dragged my feet towards the exit.

The condition of my illness persisted. My mother lost the confidence he had with medical doctors. Her commitment to Christianity notwithstanding, she forcefully suggested that we should consult a traditional doctor. So I was prepared to see a fifth doctor.

We rose up very early the following morning. We boarded a mini-bus that took us to Kitalalifu village. From there we walked on foot for about ten kilometres to a village at the foot of the Livingstone Mountains. We reached the doctor's homestead. It constituted of three huts and a *shamba* of banana and coffee.

The doctor was a skinny old man, certainly in his late seventies. He could hardly walk. He was apparently senile and he coughed constantly. Despite the coughing he lit his pipe and smoked profusely. The coughing seemed to be a problem that had been with him for a long time. It is possible it aggravated his senile condition.

My mother explained to him about my chest and throat problem. He asked me to remove my shirt. I did as I was told. Using a razor blade he cut two marks on my chest. The marks appeared like number 11 but of course in blood not ink. Then he gripped me on my shoulders and drew my chest towards his mouth. With his toothless mouth he sucked the place he had incised in me.

I felt like something coming out. Then he stopped sucking. As if chewing something then he spat on a banana leaf. It was a piece of a bone the size of a ludo dice. The bone was coated with blood and some greenish stuff that looked like leaves.

I did not touch the piece of bone and I did not believe that it came out of my body. The doctor asked my mother to pay him some money. I could not guess how much he asked for. Without hesitating, my mother untied a knot of her khanga where she had safely kept the money. She took some of it and in a squatted position she stretched her hand to give the money to the doctor. He received the money. He paused for a while and asked her to add some more. Without bargaining my mother once more untied her khanga knot and took out some money and handed it to him.

The "minor operation" done by the traditional doctor did not give me the relief I expected. The problem persisted. In July 1979 I travelled to the town by the Great Lake. I was to live there for two years. While there I decided to consult a sixth doctor. So I visited the Regional Hospital. I went through the registration procedures for outpatients.

I was directed by a nurse to a consultation room. I joined other patients who were sitting at a mahogany bench outside the room. People went in one by one. Eventually it was my turn to go in. The doctor was a person in his middle age, comparatively younger than the other doctors I had consulted previously. His hair was uncombed and he had beards on his chin. He wore a dark blue shirt with some buttons undone. This exposed his hairy chest.

I explained to him what my problem was and the history of the illness. He did not say anything. As he was about to prescribe for me his secretary interrupted him. She had been typing something then she came across a word she could not read. She wanted the doctor to spell the word for her. The doctor examined the draft and he said the word was "tremor". He spelt it out for her. Then he prescribed my medication, handed me the card and directed me to the pharmacy section. The pharmacist took some time to wrap small parcels of medicines for me. I collected the parcels and headed to a place I lived.

While in my room I opened each parcel. There were different types of medicines. I differentiated them by colours, shape and size. They were capsules, tablets and pills. Some tablets were bigger than those I had taken before. I had to break them into four pieces in order to swallow them.

I finished the dose as per prescription but there was no improvement. I decided to visit the hospital and consult another doctor. He would be the seventh doctor. A friend of mine introduced me to him. He was acquainted to him. I expected that to be an opportunity for me. I expected that he would keenly listen to me. I believed that if he would be able to understand the problem he would also be able to prescribe the right medicine.

He was a young doctor in specs. His height was not more than five feet. He had on high heeled shoes and maintained neat and fine long hairs. My friend and I met him on the corridor while we were going to his office. During the introduction he was looking at me searchingly as if he was trying to establish something. When my friend had finished the introduction I explained the problem. His immediate reaction was: "Why bring to me a chronic case?" The tone showed his sarcasm to me.

I drew a conclusion that he was least concerned. The term "chronic" he used to describe my condition disappointed me. I lost trust in the medicine even before he prescribed it for me.

I was still standing in the corridor when he wrote the prescription. For the second time I left the hospital with several parcels of different types of medicine. I do not remember if I took any of those drugs.

In July 1981 I joined National Service at KJ. Before joining the service brother Daniel had told me that on the first day I would go through "introduction to the camp." By this he said "they will make you run around the camp with your bag on your back." Thus while walking to the camp gate, considering my asthmatic condition I was not sure if I would cope with the "introduction to camp." "Welcome," said the soldier who was on sentry at the gate. He relieved me with the bag. I didn't believe. I thought "he must be fooling me the introduction to the camp would be coming soon." He took me to the receiving coy where I was equally kindly received. Later my name was slotted into B Company where I got acquainted with a fellow recruit. He had just graduated from a medical college and attained a qualification as a Medical Assistant. He told me that during the graduation ceremony he was announced the best student. He scooped all the seven prizes offered by the college.

He was to be my eighth doctor. One night I explained to him about the illness that had troubled me for the past two years. He said that he would check me the following morning. In the morning we went out of the hangar. The sun was just rising from the East. Using a table spoon he pressed my tongue. He asked me to say "*aah*" so that he could examine my throat. After a minute the exercise was over. He said: "As I suspected, you have hypertrophic tonsils." I asked him what that meant. He said that it meant that my tonsils were larger than the normal size. I further asked him what would be the cure. He replied "The only cure I know is tonsillectomy." Again I had to ask what that meant. "It is the removal of the tonsils by surgical means. You can call it minor operation but it has to be done by an ENT specialist," he elaborated. I came to learn that ENT stood for Ear Nose and Throat.

Within that week I started the procedure to consult the ENT specialist. The procedure had to begin with the National Service doctor, the District Medical Officer and the Regional Surgeon.

Thus I proceeded to the ninth doctor. This was the DMO. My friend escorted me to see him. He had known the doctor before the day we went there. We met the DMO in one of the hospital pavements. He was a tall handsome person. I got to know that he attained his MD degree in Western Europe. I envied him in his blue jeans. He looked confident and relaxed. He was jovial and approachable. His drooping moustache reminded me of Lech Walesa, leader of the reform movement in Poland. He invited us in his office. He studied the medical sheet I carried with me from the KJ. Then he listened to what my friend explained. He asked me to open my mouth. He looked at my throat and confirmed that I had hypertrophic tonsils. The following day I got a referral letter from his office to the Regional Surgeon. The letter was short; three sentences hardly covering a quarter of a page. But the letter was enough to make me get a pass from the KJ Adjutant.

Having obtained the pass I travelled to the Regional Hospital, where I was admitted.

I had informed my parents that I may be operated as the only way to cure the tonsillitis problem. They sent my brother Daniel to come to the hospital to see me. He came and found me outside the ward. I was eating a peach. Before even greeting me he said jokingly, "Friend, I thought you were sick how come a sick person eats a peach like that?" Daniel stayed with me for a short while then he begged to leave. I escorted him to the exit gate.

Before we reached the gate we met, the Regional Surgeon. He was coming from the theatre. What a coincidence! Daniel and the doctor knew each other. They had met before. So Daniel introduced me to him. He looked very polite and he spoke softly. I had heard patients at the hospital talking good things about him.

He was, for example, known for working for long hours. His principle was that he must attend all the patients who had come for service for each particular day. Being the only surgeon in the region he had long queues of patients.

The surgeon was to be my tenth doctor in the series of doctors I had consulted. He said he had been informed about my problem. He said he could perform the operation but the problem was lack of appropriate equipment. Without the proper equipment there was a risk of the operation not being very successful. "An unsuccessful tonsillectomy may cause you a permanent coarse voice," he said without hesitation. You will have to see the ENT specialist at the major referral hospital." He insisted.

Thus I was to see the eleventh doctor. I went to the referral hospital ENT department. That was January 1982. After queuing for several hours I went in the consultation room. I met a team of doctors. I presented the problem. I learned that the doctor who led the discussion was known as a consultant. But I could not follow what they were discussing. The consultant had a heavy voice. He looked confident and superior. The consultant seemed to be pouring his knowledge to the members of the group. He directed that I should visit the clinic a month later.

In February 1982 I went to the hospital as per the appointment. I sat at the bench outside the ENT clinic room. This time I did not enter the consultation room. A male nurse took my file to the doctors. After an hour he brought me a card. I had been given another appointment. I was to attend the clinic after one month.

I went home very disappointed. The pain in the throat and the breathing difficulties were worsening.

On the date for the appointment I went to the clinic. The consultant was not there. Another doctor was leading other doctors in the discussion. He looked at my card. They discussed amongst themselves. When they were about to write another postponement, the male nurse intervened. He looked at me. I looked at him. I could see the image of my father on his face. My eyes were filled with tears. The male nurse gathered courage. He said: "no" to the doctors with regard to the postponement. "This young man has had the operation postponed two times already. How can you postpone for the third time?" He lamented.

The new team leader, the twelfth doctor, agreed with what the male nurse proposed. I was led to the operating theatre in May 1982. The operation was carried out successfully and I did not experience a coarse voice.

I looked back at the history of the illness that made me suffer for three years. I was at last free from the illness. I felt indebted to the fellow recruit at KJ who made the correct diagnosis. That was when my journey to a body and mind free from the humiliation of the illness started. I also felt indebted to that male nurse whose fatherly concern blocked another postponement of the operation. The fatherly image of the nurse has always remained with me.

Moreover, the experience taught me a lesson that the right diagnosis doesn't have to come from the most senior medic. However, the experience made me become aware and appreciate the role of specialists in the medical profession.

CHAPTER 12

"THE DEITIES OF OLYMPUS" UNMASKED

Following the application that I had submitted to the university at "Hill," towards the end of 1983, I received an admission letter for the academic year that was to start in July 1984. Through the media I learned that the history of the Hill was punctuated by incidences of students' strikes. These would sometimes lead to the closure of the university. I heard that at one time the situation at the Hill deteriorated so much that the editor of the students' bulletin had this headline: 'The Crumbling Olympus'.

Before I joined the Hill, I did not know what Olympus was. Thus when I joined there I was very curious to know what it was.

Majoring in Literature I had courses that included African Literature, African American and Caribbean Literature, Literature and Revolution and others.

Among the books we studied included the well-known *Things Fall Apart* by Chinua Achebe and *The Interpreters* by Wole Soyinka. In African American and Caribbean Literature, we among other things, studied Richard Wright's *Black Boy, Native Son* and James Baldwin's *Fire Next Time*. In Literature and Revolution course, one of the major readings was Mikhail Sholokhov's *Virgin Soil Upturned*. Time for optional reading was very limited but I tried to read Leo Tolstoy's *War and Peace*. One of the major characters in the book was Napoleon Bonaparte. He reminded me of the days at the Precious Stone Town primary school when we consulted what we believed was his oracle book. I had consulted the 'book' on several occasions including when checking whether Kipusa loved me or not. Baldwin's title was seen as an allusion of the Biblical story that after the flood no more water but fire next time. None of the books I have mentioned, however, included narration about the Olympus.

It was in the course of Theories of Literature where the lectures included reference to the Greek mythology. It was from those lectures that I learned of the Greek legends mostly used by the poet

Homer to write *The Iliad and Odyssey*. I also became aware how the myths seemed to have influenced many novelists. For example, I became aware of tragic heroes in the novels I read. I could link the novels to the myths when it came to the concept of tragedy and the qualities of a hero.

Through the course I was also able to learn that Olympus was a name of a mountain. In the Greek mythology the mountain was believed to be the home of the deities. The deities were under their "chief" called Zeus, who was also believed to be the father of mortals.

The University being situated on a hill and Olympus being a mountain must have been the reason for the editor of the students' bulletin to employ the metaphor: Olympus for the hill, hence the headline 'The Crumbling Olympus' when he described the situation at the University.

Our lecturer also shed light on Homer's hero, Odysseus. He particularly focused on the episode where the hero tricked the Trojans and captured the city of Troy. The capture of the city also led to the taking back of a woman who had been abducted by the Trojans.

Even so life at the Olympus, that is to say, the University, was generally good and courses run smoothly. It then happened that signs of discontents begun to emerge when I was in my third year. The students were unhappy with the way the administration run things. Students believed that the administration had sufficient funds to offer us a better menu and out of pocket allowance than it was offering. The students also believed that the administration could have done something to resolve the chronic water problem and shortage of chairs in the seminar rooms. Tea cups were also in serious shortage.

We boycotted classes under cover of the so-called extended school *Baraza* (Council). The *Baraza* was allowed constitutionally. There were several closed sessions between students' leaders and the university administration in the council chamber. Agenda was moved from the chamber to the open *Baraza* in the assembly hall. I did not hold any leadership position but I attended all the meetings that were held in the assembly hall.

In one of the meetings held in the hall, the students' leaders alleged that the administration was misappropriating funds. Whatever that meant it became the official position of the students. They argued that there was no other explanation for the poor menu and the extent to which other services were lacking. On their side the administrators claimed that they tried to convince the government to increase the budget but the government kept saying NO! NO! NO!

The students, on the other hand, insisted on their demands. The pressure seemed to have pushed the administration to look for funds by all means. In a few days, since the extended *Baraza* begun, the situation somewhat improved at the Hill. However, the improvements could not be sustained for long. After a while the situation deteriorated again.

"Politics" was not only between the students and the administration but also among students themselves. There was a secret society whose leader was only referred to as *Mzee* (the Old man). Through the writings he now and then posted on the cafeteria wall he claimed that 'he was omnipotent, that he was 'the chief deity' at the Hill.

Whoever *Mzee* was, the truth was that, he succeeded in building fear in the students' community. The students believed that 'the chief deity' was capable of knowing anything taking place at the "Olympus and beyond". *Mzee* himself boasted of being omnipresent yet invisible. It was clear that he was not alone. He must have "the lesser deities" working for him.

Mzee and his "lesser deities" seized the power to 'correct' others through wall literature. They 'published' things that portrayed all the negatives of a person. The purpose of their publication was to embarrass the targeted person and belittle him or her. The placards that contained the 'dirty' literature were posted at night and people saw them in the morning. *Mzee's* "editors" specialized in character assassination.

I perceived *Mzee* as a bully just like those form twos at Levavi Oculos or Usukile Pabandu at FDS in the Precious Stone Town. The only difference was that he operated at a higher education level and in a more secretive way.

One morning, students found out *Mzee's* boys had published bad things about a lady who was otherwise liked because she was very charming, bold, daring and friendly to most students at the Hill.

The lady did not accept the humiliation. She was not ready to see her character easily 'assassinated'. Thus, in broad daylight she retaliated by posting a strong statement against *Mzee* and his boys. She dared mention some names of the boys and their halls of residence. That was the first time ever that someone had publicly confronted and challenged *Mzee*.

Previously, a myth prevailed that *Mzee* was invincible and unchallenged. The bold lady broke the myth. Since then *Mzee's* boys looked like toothless dogs. Their deity had been stripped off them. *Mzee*, 'the chief deity', of the Olympus was no longer omnipotent; he had been defeated and suffered humiliation in the hands of this bold lady.

What the lady did could be likened to the episode in *Things Fall Apart* when Enoch, a Christian Convert in Umuofia, unmasked an *egwugwu* in public (the *egwugwu* were clan elders who masked themselves to assume the status of the immortal spirits of the ancestors. By unmasking one of them proved that the *egwugwu* were not the immortal ancestors but the mortal clan elders).

Some weeks after the incident that embarrassed *Mzee*, the 'deities' came up with another publication. As usual it was posted on the walls of the cafeteria. People ignored it and it did not seem to carry the weight the previous 'publications' had before the de mystification of the deities.

Finally, the issue to me was not whether the "chief deity" and the "lesser deities" were right or wrong but it was the courage demonstrated by the lady to confront them in the broad daylight, openly and single-handedly!

I completed my studies at Olympus in third week of May 1987. The studies, among other things, had imparted in me a passion for reading, particularly reading novels based on true stories.

CHAPTER 13

END OF AN ERA

One morning of May 1987 the church bell rang. This was meant to communicate a message that a member of the congregation had passed away. The person who had died was none other than my father, the man who had ministered the congregation for a quarter of a century.

For twenty-five years he had served his people. This is the man who after the Sunday service would not head home but visit the sick and the elderly. His love for his people enabled him to command a lot of respect and to receive a lot of love too from the people he cared.

The news of his death spread like fire on a grass-thatched roof. Then there was a blanket of silence that covered the land.

Before he passed away my father had written me his last letter. He wrote to inform me that he was ill. He got ill at the mid of a land conflict. The conflict involved the traditionalist and the members of the congregation. The controversial issue was the land on which the church building stood. Many efforts to resolve the conflict did not bear good fruits. I suspected that he overstretched himself and the stress overpowered him.

To a certain degree the conflict had some aspects that seemed similar to the ones portrayed by Ngugi wa Thiong'o in *The River Between*. Naturally I equated my father to Joshua, the leader of the Christian community in Kameno, in Ngugi's book. I remembered the words Joshua said: "But for me and my house, we will serve the Lord." I would not hesitate to put the same words into my father's mouth and heart.

In the letter he wrote it was clear that he neither hoped nor desired to live any longer.

One evening in May, he passed away. The sun had just set beyond Nyika Mountains. At the foot of the Mountain lay my grandmother's village. The light of the sun seemed to have drifted away so swiftly while it was still desired. The news of the death continued spreading from one ridge to the next. All the paths in the ridges led to our home.

The following day the old man was laid to rest. Soon after they finished burying the body there came a heavy downpour. The deacon commented, "It is not raining but pouring." Two boys had taken shelter under a banana tree, as they could not get a place inside the house for it was full of mourners.

"This was a great man," said one of the boys.

"Why?" asked the other boy.

"The heavy rain that is pouring tells it all," answered the other boy.

The following Sunday a sermon was held at the home of the old man as it was the custom of the church. The priest who led the sermon introduced the subject of the day: "Let us be prepared for the life here after.". The priest made a long sermon. When he was through he invited church elders to speak something. The first speaker was a well known church elder. He was especially known for his loud and clear voice. "I was suffering from a toothache but when I heard the news about the death I could not feel the pain anymore. However, soon after the burial my pain was back," he lamented.

Things did not remain the same for the hundred and fifty congregators. The leadership vacuum was soon filled with something different. They could not congregate under one roof as they used to do. They split and took different directions. Some went eastward. Others went westward and joined a congregation that had been established there. Some did not like to join any of the new congregations. They planted the church where it did not exist before.

When my father died I was twenty-eight. I had already secured a job as a teacher but it was painful to me that the man who sent me to school did not live to see me as a university graduate. Daniel had been a civil servant for nine years. I looked at him and I did not doubt at all that I could count on him. Thus it did not ring in my mind that I should worry. However, I could not resist worrying for my mother. I was overwhelmed by the instincts that without my father the village was no longer a safe place for her. To me my father was the chief protector of my mother. Before Daniel and my younger brothers and sisters: Abel Chrissdom, Suma and Sekela, my uncle was there too. I argued: "Our mother should go and stay with the grandmother in Ilalabwe."

My uncle rejected the proposal and my mother too objected. They had different reasons but it all meant the same that my mother would remain in the village. My uncle argued that my mother had always been there and God had been her protector.

When it was her turn to speak she said that she would not run away from her husband. I clearly heard her saying, "Should I run away from Baba Dani?" (My mother always preferred Dani to Daniel when referring to or calling my brother). To her my father was dead but his spirit was present right there in our home.

By this thinking it was no wonder that a flask full of tea with milk was set aside for my father throughout the days of the funeral. I could not understand this. I asked my aunt (the elder sister of my father), who took care of that item, why they were doing that. They were Christians anyway. She told me that my father had been coming to them through dreams. When they did not keep some tea for him he came and complained that he was hungry. "But the tea that you kept for him is still in the flask?" I asked. "Yes it is still there but it has gone bad already. That is the indicator that he drunk it." She answered. By the same belief she tuned to "*Sauti ya Injili*" (the Voice of the Gospel) because my father used to listen to the Radio station broadcasting from its base in Moshi. Thus even so he was dead, they believed, he still listened to the programme.

My father's funeral provided a lesson for me on what my people believed about life after death. During my childhood I heard my parents talking about the living ancestors, *nsyuka*. But I never thought that one day my own father would be *nsyuka*. Most interesting to me were the claims made by some elders, including prominent figures in the local church, that he had been visiting them through their dreams. Some even claimed that God had been talking to them. They added that God was heard saying that His servant had died before he finished the work he was called to do.

While the multitude was mourning for the untimely death of my father, there was an old woman at the other side of the village. She wished she were the one who was dead. She was suffering from a disease related to the respiratory system. One could hear her breathing with so much difficult

and in much pain. She had been bed ridden
for many years.

On the occasions I paid her a visit,
she would complain against the ancestors
for not 'opening the door to let her in'.
"*Bangalalileki* (why are they angry with
me?" She would ask staring at nothing. Her
case reminded me of old Boshof in Peter
Godwin's *Mukiwa*. Boshof, one of the
last pioneers of Rhodesia, suffering from
impaired breathing, wished his death. Apart
from buying his own coffin, he on a number
of times, just imagined that he was already
dead and declared so while in reality he was
still alive. He once told a doctor attending to
him, "Next time, I really will die."

My mother and close relatives mourned
my father for thirty days. But sympathizers
continued to visit my mother several months
later. She never left the home she established
with her husband. My young brothers Abel
and Chrissdom attended the banana trees all
around our home. They also looked after the
cows.

Daniel and I returned to Dar es Salaam
in June 1987.

CHAPTER 14

UNDERNEATH THE ENDURANCE

God bless our School,

Leaders and students,
Long live our school,
God bless teachers,
And the workers,
Let us maintain the Motto,
Act without being pushed.

Our School is situated,
Beside a hill and beside a road,
Long live our school.

So was the anthem of the school where I went to teach on my first appointment as a teacher in a Southern district. I was there in the morning assembly when the students sung. I was in a pink long sleeves shirt, blue jeans trousers and rubber shoes. My dressing was different from what made me envy my bush school teacher twenty two years previously. Dressing like my former teacher: white short sleeve shirt, white shorts and white socks I believed was out of fashion.

"I will be teaching literature in English and English Language," I said in my introduction to the students. Some students murmured. Those who did not do so wore frowned faces. "Isn't literature the same as English," one of them shouted. Others applauded, though not so loudly. My fellow teachers looked at me with raised eye brows. "I will tell you the difference in class," I replied.

In the class, I explained that in Literature we would have readings to study such as *Things Fall Apart* by Chinua Achebe. "While in the English subject we will look at the structure of the English language," I added. But the students did not seem to be enthusiastic to learn the subjects. To raise their interest in the subjects, I started a school newsletter I called "The Fortnight Review." In creating the title I was influenced by *Weekly Review*, a magazine that was published in Nairobi. The writers for the newsletter were the students themselves. They submitted many articles. I edited and "published" them in the newsletter. Most of the students wrote on sports, dances and other social events. I could feel a sense of satisfaction and the meaning of my work.

Study hours were however disturbed by a chronic water shortage. In comparison to the schools I had been as a student, the school in the south was small. It had about half the number of students compared to Levavi Oculos. But there wasn't enough water for them. The shortage was more serious even if compared to the school by the Great Lake. Students wandered in surrounding areas and even away from the school looking for water. Students would take bath using half of a ten litre bucket.

One day the school matron presented a case before the staff members that Alimaso, one of the watchmen, saw two girls at a house next to his, about three kilometres from the school. "The watchmen says the girls were with two young men," the matron said. "Is this true," we asked the girls, standing before us. "It is true the watchman saw us when we were looking for water. We even had our buckets with us," the girls said while sobbing. None of us was convinced, anyway. We ruled that they should be suspended.

I left the staff room. I further thought about our decision. "It might be true that the girls were looking for water and those two young men, had enough water in their home and were ready to help as mere sympathizers of the girls' situation. But it could also be true the young men and the girls were lovers and the girls took the water shortage as advantage to get permission to get into town and meet them," I thought.

As a teacher I was privileged to get two buckets of water every morning. It was the duty of the head girl to assign two girls to carry a bucket each to my house. The two buckets were, however, not enough. I had to use a quarter of a bucket of water for bathing. I used water which remained after washing clothes, to flush toilets. And I watered a few tomato plants in my kitchen garden with water saved after washing dishes.

In an unusual situation, one day the head girl did not assign any girl to take water to Madam Binti, a thin female teacher who had just joined the school staff team. She reported the matter to the headmistress and the head girl was suspended. I took trouble to do my own investigation to find out why was it that the head girl did such a thing.

Luckily, I overheard the girls conversing: "Madam Binti is just a girl like us how can we fetch water for her?" I was disturbed. I didn't report to the headmistress of what I found. I feared that the headmistress might decide to punish the head girl even further. "What the girls didn't know or pretended not to know was that by being thin it didn't mean Madam Binti was not older than them. After all, she was a teacher and she deserved to be receive two buckets of water like any other teacher," I thought. Never the less I thought the suspension was too much of a punishment for such a wrong.

Besides coping with the water shortage, the students had to endure the safari to the school when they were coming from holiday. In January 1988 I was assigned to escort students from Songea to the school and I experienced what the travel meant.

"Teacher, let us take some male passengers. The road is muddy and slippery. We are going to need them to push the bus," so said to me the driver of the bus that the school had hired to take the students from Songea. I agreed. We allowed about eight men to join us. We left Songea for Tunduru at around 9.00 am. It was the beginning of a nearly 270 kilometre journey.

From Songea to Namtumbo it was relatively plain and we drove smoothly. Then the road went through a terrain with several steep hills with muddy clay soil. And our journey was punctuated by a lot of pushing the bus out of the wet and sticky clay soil. Several times we had to disembark, roll our trousers, remove our shoes and push the bus. The girls disembarked from the bus too and pushed the bus. In some cases men dug for dry sand off the road and the girls carried it to the muddy spot. The dry sand put on the muddy spot helped to dry it and make it less slippery. The bus went up and down of so many hills. The road largely passed through a virgin forest. There was a good distance from one village to next. On both sides of the road, to the farthest point the eyes could see there was no sign of human life. I suspected human feet had never treaded some of the places in the area. It was the toughest safari I had ever had.

We arrived at Tunduru at round 8.00pm in the evening. We stopped there for a rest. The journey was to continue the following day and it would take us six hours to reach our destination. Tunduru was infamous for man-eating lions. Mysterious lions grabbed their targeted victims even at the centre of the town. The lions did not wait to be hunted. They attacked the hunters even before the victims planned their expeditions in the jungle. The rumours went that the man who "made" the lions, came from a distant land. They had it that the man brought some fish in order to sell them at the Tunduru market. He had to walk for three days to get there. Then it was said that the man complained that some people stole his fish. Then the man-made lions came targeting the very people who had stolen the fish. The lion, so it was said, dragged some victims from the Tunduru market into the bush in broad daylight. I suspected that the people of East Africa had not heard a story of man-eating lions similar to that of the lions of Tsavo. Then there came the lions of Tunduru!

The students who used the route were the last to arrive at the school. Students from other districts, which had alternative routes to reach the school, had already arrived. Our bus approached the school. Their fellow students cheered. One could see tears of joy in both the arriving students and the welcoming ones.

But "every cloud has a silver lining". Despite of the upsetting water shortage, the disturbing suspensions and the difficult travel, the South is where I met Stella, who later became my better half. Until then I did not believe in the adage: love at first sight. But I happened to love her at my very first glance. It was from that encounter that we continued contacting each other until we married. Our wedding took place on 13th August 1994 in Dar es Salaam.

On 18th March 1995 we were blessed with a baby boy. We named him Lugano, meaning 'love' in Kinyakyusa. On 8th June 1998, we were again blessed with another baby boy. We named our newly born baby boy Elisha.

CHAPTER 15

LEARNING PARALLELED ILLNESS

Towards the end of 1990 I started feeling sick. At night I sweated a lot; the bed sheets got wet as if soaked into water. And I noticed that I was losing weight. I took for granted that it would be malaria. I took some anti malaria tablets but I did not feel any better. Then I thought that a change of scene would end the illness. So I travelled to my home village. During my stay in the village I visited my father's elder brother. As I was greeting him he stared at me. "You must be sick. I can see the illness," he shouted while holding my hand. "Yes I feel a bit sick but I have taken some medicine and I hope I will be ok," I replied. Then he shouted again: "The disease is still in your body." I felt embarrassed. I wondered how he knew that I was sick. I however, appreciated his knowledge.

The following day I sat at a ground in front of our house, where I used to sit and gaze at the horizon. It was a bright morning with a sunshine that provided comforting warmth and I was reading *Have a Change of Scene* by James Hadley Chase. "Good morning," a man passing by greeted me. "Good morning," I replied while putting the novel aside. He stopped and stared at me. "You must be sick. Aren't you," he said in a low voice. I could not find words to reply. I forced a smile. After two days I told my mother that I would like to leave for Dar es Salaam. "Didn't you say that you would stay with us for two weeks?" She asked in a high tone. "I might have said so but…," I replied but fumbled for words. "Okay," she replied. Then I travelled to Dar es Salaam by bus. My health condition did not improve; I was feverish and vomited immediately after eating. I went to a referral hospital where I was admitted for several days.

I was first discharged then readmitted. The doctors said that I had presented an interesting case. Whatever that meant but the issue to me was that I was sick. I had never been hospitalized for so long before. The diagnosis stage took a long time to complete. I moved from one doctor to another, from one laboratory to the next. I attended one clinic after another.

After almost a year of investigation, doctors finally came to establish that I was suffering from a plastic anemia. As a result of the disease I became anemic. I suffered from blood deficiency. The Hematologist, who attended me, told me that for the case to be reversible I must be very lucky. There was the probability of the case being irreversible. He said that should that happen I would be suffering from chronic blood deficiency. He told me the disease was a side effect of a drug I had used. The drug affected the marrow. The Hematologist said something I cannot recall about the connection between the marrow and the red blood cells. Thus he had to establish how to proceed with the treatment after testing the marrow.

I was informed one day before the marrow test. The night before the operation I could not sleep. I was not afraid of the operation for I had undergone several tests before. I kept pondering how the doctor would extract the marrow from my bones. Basing on my secondary school biology my understanding was that the marrow is found inside the bones. How would the doctor extract it?

I hardly slept that night. It was not so much because of fear but rather I tried to theorise how the doctors would obtain the bone marrow from my body.

On the day of the operation I was taken into the theatre on a wheel chair. The theatre was not like the one where Dr Weiti had operated me many years before, when I was a student at Precious Stone Town. This one was more of a laboratory. The doctor was there waiting for me. He asked me to sit on a bed. The bed had a mattress as hard as a soft wood. He instructed me to remove my shirt and face the other side so he was behind me. I was there tense and waiting. I began doubting all my theories. Later all my theories were proved wrong. The doctor did not apply any of them.

I was facing the wall so I did not see what he held in his hand. I could only intelligently guess that it was a syringe connected to a sharp and strong needle. He injected the needle somewhere on the waist. The operation continued for about half an hour.

After the marrow test the doctors confirmed that I was suffering from a plastic anaemia. I remained in the hospital for about three weeks on the third floor of the hospital. I was not bed ridden but the nurses restricted my movements. They warned me that my immunity was not strong enough so I had to avoid unnecessary interaction with other patients and visitors.

During the three weeks or so that I stayed at the hospital ward my two cousins, Tupokigwe and Isengela, brought me food of my taste. They came to the third floor ward twice or thrice a day. Their great care for me was a testimony of deep affection. Throughout the days that I was hospitalized I never felt abandoned because of them.

I was discharged from the hospital. But I was to continue with a long treatment as an outpatient. I was required to take medicine every day for the whole year. The arrangement was that every Monday I would collect tablets at the clinic for the whole week. I was to take tablets everyday without fail. I was also advised to eat a balanced diet.

The doctor was not very specific on what I had to eat but people, who had suffered from a similar health problem before, strongly advised me to take a glass of milk every day. Brother Daniel, whom I stayed with during the period of recovery, arranged with a milk supplier for a litre per day. The supplier never failed.

In addition to the tablets, I was to have intra muscular injections of the prescribed medicine for sixty days. I also learnt that the injections were to be administered through the veins (intra vein). But only a few nurses then could administer the injection in this way. My cousin, Tupokigwe, who had become a nurse herself, arranged with a male nurse to inject me at home. The man came for the sixty days without fail. The milk and the injection arrangements went very well.

For the whole year when I was under medication and excused from duty the care and love I received from my relatives is invaluable. I was not idle during the fifteen months of the sick leave. I had a lot of informal education from various people who came to visit me. I received many visitors, but of all these, two were outstanding: Rastafari and Rock.

Rastafari said that he was dedicated to bringing back to Zion the remnants still under captivity in Babylon. For me Babylon was a mere ancient civilization, but for Rastafari Babylon was a general term for the corrupt world. Understanding Rastafari was not easy. He even had his own vocabulary. For example, there were words, which he never used. Words like 'but', 'understand', could not be found in his vocabulary. The word 'understand' was substituted with the word 'over stand'. Rastafari claimed that he was always above the situation not under the situation. And often he said to me: "Don't worry brother the illness will be over."

The 'I' had a very special meaning to him. It conveyed the feelings of his heart. It meant oneness or togetherness. So instead of saying you and I, Rastafari would say I and I. In this way the word 'me' was also eliminated. Instead of me, he would say 'I man'.

'My' and 'mine' were also eliminated in his vocabulary. So instead of saying, for example, my book he would say 'I man book'. The word 'reasoning' was used instead of 'discussing'.

Rastafari's 'Teachings' gave me new insights. He had something new every time. Like a good teacher he did not rush his student. His lessons ranged from personal names to the history of Black African people.

As far as names are concerned, his principle was that Africans should reclaim their names. He said that African names had meanings. Calling an African name invoked certain spirits. In Africa names were not labels, he insisted.

For the entire period he visited me not a single day did I see him without a stick and a suitcase. For the stick he said he had to carry it because Moses (from the Bible) carried a stick. In his suitcase he always carried a Bible and a manuscript of a book he was trying to write. For the Bible he always read the Old Testament especially the books of Moses, Isaiah and Psalms. Frankly speaking, when he read the verses he selected, it was as if I had never read the Bible before. His central reference was the blessings and the curse as written in Deuteronomy Chapter 28. The theme formed the foundation of his teachings. Even in the book he was trying to write he pursued the same theme.

He built up the plot for the theme by making numerous quotations from several books in the Bible. Why of course not a book from the New Testament was quoted. Apart from the Bible he heavily quoted *The African Origin of Civilization Myth or Reality* by C. A.

Diop. The other 'great' book that Rastafari had was *Nile Valley Civilization* by Ivan Van. In my opinion, these two books should be must reads for African students, particularly, those studying History and Political Science.

My interaction with Rastafari proved to me that I was ignorant of the Bible and Africa. Rastafari told me that the word Egypt appears seven hundred and twenty times in the Bible. He asserted that Moses was not only married to an African woman but also learned about delegation from his father-in-law. Thus, according to Rastafari, the Bible has an African origin. He argued that the problem was that most of us were not taught to read the Bible in the right perspective.

I was even confused to learn from the encyclopedia he once lent me that the laws in the Pentateuch were very similar to the Babylonian Assyrian religious laws. Interestingly, the religion existed many years before the Biblical Moses, to whom the Pentateuch is attributed. He claimed that he was a servant of one and true living God. When I told him I also believed in the one and true living God, he did not agree with what I said. He pointed out that I and many others were followers of other gods and that was why we had not received the blessings.

Rastafari's teachings were not confined to the Bible. He also covered other subjects like food, politics and clothes. He often warned me that he did not like what I ate. He suggested a completely different menu for me. Home made fresh fruit juice instead of canned or bottled industrial drinks. Brown bread was to replace white bread. Porridge was to replace tea. Brown sugar was to replace white sugar. Honey on bread instead of margarine. Vegetables were to replace red meat. Salt was not to be part of the meal.

He discouraged me from taking all types of meat including white meat and milk. He said milk was for the calf. When I asked him for example, why he could not eat pork he claimed that a pig is a sick animal. I must admit that I cannot rule out his influence on my food habits. Since then I have never omitted fruits in my menu. Rastafari emphasized that there was a strong relationship between what one eats and his or her health. His bottom line argument was that wrong food was like wrong oil into a motorcar.

Our conversations were spontaneous; we jumped from one topic to another. Besides discussing about food we spend time discussing politics. Some names came out often and Rastafari spoke positively of them. The names included Marcus Garvey, Peter Tosh, Steve Biko and Walter Rodney. He actually called them prophets. He lent me several books written by those he called prophets. One such books was entitled *The Philosophy of Marcus Garvey*. The book, among other things, covered extensively on Garvey's "Back to Africa" initiative. The initiative saw the establishment of the Black Star Shipping Line.

However, political reasoning did not take Rastafari away from his fundamental argument that Africans experienced hardships because they had not received the blessings. We would reason for a long time then he would say! "Hold on brother, this is more than academics, it is more than politics, it is more than economics, it is spiritual." He argued that unless our people started tackling our problems from a spiritual point of view, the current problems would not be solved. He strongly spoke of Africa for every black African. He thus exhorted that there was no need for an African to carry a passport when he crossed frontiers within Africa.

When it came to colour of clothes, Rastafari had his preference: Yellow, Green, Red, and Black and sometimes Grey. He always put on black or brown sandals. I liked the man. He was humble, respectful, generous and very caring. He would rather give than receive. He would be quick to note a person who was in need and rush to assist. He had a very positive attitude, respect and love for a black woman. He also loved children.

When it was time for him to go he would say "Brother, peace be with you." Rastafari's ultimate goal was to build what he called the city of habitation. He kept the map of the city next to his Bible in his suitcase. The city of habitation when completed would be an ideal city. Free from the influence of Babylon.

One day Rastafari told me that the time had come for him to leave for the land of river Malagarasi where he would construct the city of habitation. I visited his home in the commercial city before he left for Malagarasi. It was a relatively small house. There were no chairs at the sitting room. We sat on a mat. "This is my queen," he said as his wife gave me a glass of lemon juice.

Rastafari had also shared his vision to build the city of habitation with C.L.R. James, a famous writer in the Caribbean. He still recalled how C.L.R. James was excited by the idea and he immediately picked a phone in order to call one of the international mass media. He wanted to involve the media in raising fund for the construction of the city of habitation.

When Rastafari asked him why the media should be involved, he quoted C.L.R. James saying: "You can't do big things in a small way."

What C.L.R. James said proved to be correct, at least by the time I visited (many years later) the site that Rastafari had attempted to develop, not much had been done.

Rock was also a special visitor in his own right. He came often to see me and we discussed many things. The discussions were particularly hot when Rock and Rastafari happened to visit me on the same day, same hour.

The two had different perspectives and the gap was enormous. For example, while

Rastafari was against non-African names, Rock did not have a problem with that. Sometimes they would debate for so long and finally Rastafari would withdraw from the debate with a statement: "The problem is that brother Rock does not even know that he is under a curse!"

One day Rock met a friend who provided him with a new insight. He, Rock's friend, told him about things called plains. According to him the one we lived in was a physical plain, while there were seven other plains. When one dies so the story went on, he goes to the second plain. The determinant factor for which plain one goes is his or her conduct here on earth. The persons who were spiritually clean went to higher plains. The story claimed cleaner persons, with some kind of training, could travel through the seven plains. The condition was that one must be able to separate his body from his soul because it is the soul, which travels. The body and soul would be reunited at the end of the journey.

Rock's friend claimed that he himself could separate his soul from his body and travel up to the fourth plain. It was said that there was only one person, under the sun, who could travel to the seventh plain.

It was very difficult to understand these things. Every time when I thought I knew, a new thing emerged and I could realize that I did not know as many things as I thought I knew.

Rock's insight was not the end of the story. Things became more complicated than they were before. Rastafari brought materials, which claimed that men in ancient Africa believed that they had seven souls. It was only one of the souls (the higher soul if you like), which could be separated from the body. It had a lot of energy, which could be used constructively or destructively. The lower soul (if you like) did not have the capacity to leave the body. It was always around the body.

Before my sick leave was over I decided to read all the Gospels. I was particularly interested to discover only those words, which Jesus said. I borrowed a portable manual typewriter from Rastafari. I didn't know how to type so I used my two fingers. It took time but I was able to type only those words, which Jesus said. I extracted them from the four Gospels. I felt satisfied but soon after my sick leave my brother in law told me that I missed the "fifth Gospel;" the

Gospel according to Barnabas. I vowed to look for the Gospel and experience its form and content.

The sick leave transformed me in several ways. For example, I came to appreciate the African elements in the Bible. I noted that in the Bible, the one that Rastafari always carried with him, the African places like Egypt and Kush were highlighted. He even claimed that Egypt was mentioned in the Bible seven hundred times. Thus, he added, the word Egypt is mentioned many times than any other word in the Bible. I didn't count to prove what he claimed but I tended to believe him. I didn't know why was it that the African perspective seemed to have been hidden from me until I listened to Rastafari's teachings.

My interaction with Rastafari also transformed me on the food safety aspect. Before being a "follower" of Rastafari, I never thought that some foods contained chemicals that could be dangerous to the body.

CHAPTER 16

UNPACKING THE INFLUX

In 1994 I was particularly assigned to work
with a relief programme following an influx
of refugees into the north western part of
our country. I recall the first time when with
my colleagues, one a photographer, and I
went to the area to assess the situation. We
went on board a one-engine aircraft. The
pilot said a word of prayer. He started the
engine. The aircraft taxied on the runway.
Slowly it gained momentum, then we took
off. After forty minutes or so we were flying
over a stream of people. They were crossing
the river that made the border between the
country where the refugees were fleeing
from and our country.

The stream of people we saw constituted
the survivors, the innocent and the fugitives.
All mingled in one and were given one
blanket status they were refugees or asylum

seekers. A mere visual assessment could not tell who was who.

We landed at a small airstrip belonging to a local church. The airstrip was not well attended, as it could be easily mistaken with a village open ground. It was not well levelled. And as the aircraft was coming to a complete stop it shook as if it was going to fall apart.

A friend of ours had been waiting for us. He came forward and helped us with our baggage. We had to hurry because the aircraft could not fly back to the seaside town, where we had come from, after 3.00 pm. We hurriedly boarded our friend's Land Rover. We drove through a hilly terrain to the camp, where the people we saw while in the air were heading.

At a distance the camp looked like a collection of anthills. It was not until we had driven closer that we recognized that the 'anthills' were actually a collection of hut like structures roofed by blue sheets. It was actually a refugee camp of nearly three hundred thousand people. The streets of the 'city' had been named after the names of big town of the country of origin of the people who had streamed into it.

The streets harboured all sorts of people. As we walked from one street to another we saw people mending bicycles, repairing shoes, dressing their hair and what have you. At one spot a crippled old man was trying to light his pipe while a young white lady was busy trying to take a photograph of him. In another part of the camp we found a makeshift church and a choir singing.

At another corner someone was selling meat. We discovered that some of the animals slaughtered at the camp butchery had been stolen from the farmers in the host community. We visited a local pastor. He lamented that his big bull went missing the previous night. "In the middle of the darkness, I heard a bullet fired. I too scared to go outside. I did not move an inch," the pastor said. "I heard some movements out of my house. Then I heard people saying that nobody could stop them from taking my bull," the pastor added.

"I can see you are hosting some refugees here," I remarked.

"Yes I have a few women and children. But do you know how many are in the camp?" the pastor asked.

"I can just guess. May be a hundred thousand," I replied.

"A church relief worker told me that they are about three hundred thousand and that currently the camp has more refugees than any other in the world," the pastor revealed.

After a short pause he added: "At our airstrip small planes fly in and out throughout the day."

I turned to a child near me, "how did you arrive here," I asked him. "We walked on foot," he replied, though in a faint voice. "How long did it take you to reach here?" "Two weeks," he said. Fiddling with his fingers he added: "We only walked at night. During day time we hid ourselves." "What do you miss here," I asked him. "My friend Bobo," he sobbed. I looked into his eyes. Tears were just dropping down to his cheeks. I didn't ask any more questions.

We returned to the camp in order to make a video documentation of the situation. Children cheered at our photographer, a light skinned guy: "*komela, mzungu komela*," be courageous. And as he went on photographing they shouted: "*Mzungu anafotoa*," the Whiteman is taking photos. We visited the feeding centre. It was full of malnourished children.

While life was the way it was at the camp, businessmen and traders in the host community were making a fortune. The local market size had more than doubled. For those who had guest houses it was like a tourist high season. The occupancy rate trebled. Whatever the case, at sun set the guest houses in the town were full. The airstrip that used to receive one aircraft per month became one of the busiest airstrips in the country.

While guesthouse owners were making a fortune, local consumers were suffering. Food prices in the town rose up all of a sudden.

Our assessment mission was over. We returned to the airstrip. The pilot was waiting impatiently. He sighed with relief when he saw us back. We boarded the plane and the pilot said a word of prayer before we flew back to the seaside town.

From the visit I was able to unveil what I thought earlier that the camp would be full of helpless people waiting for donations. Instead most of the people were live and active.

CHAPTER 17

BEYOND THE BORDERS

"Welcome on board," said the flight attendant in her nasal passionate voice. That was sometimes in 1997 when I travelled on a more than nine-hours non- stop night flight by KLM flight to the North, across the Mediterranean. It was dream come true. From the days as a student at the school by the great lake, I dreamt of boarding KLM. It was the advertisement in the magazine that periodically circulated among the students that made me fascinated by the airline. The travel was a result of an invitation from a development partner. While on board I also remembered my childhood days. During that time we called "*akaroketi*, a rocket" any aircraft that crossed the sky over our village. "Now for sure I am not on board of a rocket but a jumbo jet plane," I thought.

In the morning we landed at the hub airport. As I disembarked from the plane I wished I had landed together with the old men of the Last Church in my village, who wanted to know where the sun sets. I wondered what kind of answer they would have.

After collecting my bags I passed through the immigration desk. Then as I was trying to find my way out of the airport, a police officer stopped me. We looked at each other. He had sharp eyes, a light moustache, stout and slightly bowed legs. "Can I see your passport," he demanded. I flushed out the passport from my breast pocket and gave him. He kind of snatched it from my hand. He examined for a while. Then still holding it he talked over a radio call to a person on the other end in a language I could not understand. Then I heard him say: "He is shabby." I did not agree with what he said, though I was afraid to speak it out, because I was wearing a jacket that I had bought from an expensive shop in Dar es Salaam. "What is the purpose of your visit," he asked in a heavy voice. "I am coming for a meeting sir," I replied. "Can I see the invitation letter." I produced the letter. He examined it then took it to another policeman who was sitting in a kind of booth a few metres away. The one who took the letter was looking at me while the other one examined it. Then he returned my passport and the letter. He waved his hand. I hurriedly walked towards the exit.

I took a taxi to the meeting venue. The taxi driver had a problem in locating the place. He unfolded a map and moved his index finger to trace the place. He folded the map and we drove slowly. He located the place and dropped me. "Bye bye," he said as banged the door of the boot after removing my bag.

After two days of the meeting I wanted to see the city. Someone had talked about the district with wooing lights and I thought I should visit the place. I boarded a bus for the town. In the bus I noticed that the passengers were not talking to one another. I also realized that the bus moved as if it was sliding because the road was so smooth. The bus moved and it was as if we were skiing. No sooner than I had enjoyed the ride we were in the town.

I walked around the city streets. Most houses dated back to the ancient architecture with a kind of aesthetic that touched my heart. I treaded on smooth pavements. The stones that were used to build the pavements looked like those found in the rivers I crossed to my grandmother's village.

Flowerpots hung on balconies. Flowers with shouting colours filled the atmosphere. At every corner my eyes were met with red, pink, yellow, blue and purple colours.

The town planners had, however, been clever enough. What I was seeing did not represent the entire picture of the town. The town had her other side. The town was divided in districts. Each district was unique in its own right. I had enough of the flower district. I drifted into another district, probably the most unique.

Instead of hanging flowers the district had apartments with hanging wooing coloured lights. The apartments had glass doors and behind each door stood a woman. I saw a man walking into one of the apartments. As soon as he entered a curtain was drawn. I walked down on of the streets and saw more men walking up and down gazing at women behind the glass door.

What I saw in the district was very strange to me. I blamed myself for visiting the place. But I was glad that I was not wooed to go beyond any of those glass doors and a curtain was not drawn behind my back. I walked out of the district.

In 1998 I travelled to a country in the near East. At the transit airport, I proceeded to the check in desk and surrendered my passport and the invitation letter. The letter was written in an archaic language. A number of young ladies in white shirts and black trousers one after another took charge of the check-in. I was asked a number of questions. Same questions were repeated a number of times. They seemed to ignore my earlier answers. The same question would be asked and I would give the same answer again and again.

The most interesting question was asked by one of the ladies. She was the apparent in-charge of the detail section. She wanted me to identify myself besides the papers I had. That was difficult. I told her that she should take it from me that the papers presented the authentic identification of me.

I also stated that there I was and it was me. I could not find any better way of proving that "I" was "I". When I was through with the checks I proceeded to the gate ready for boarding. After the usual safety instructions the pilot of In the Air airline, welcomed us on board. The plane took off. The flight was enjoyable. The flight attendant constantly served us with drinks and bites until we landed at the airport named after the founder of the nation-state.

Later in 1999 I made another international flight. I landed at the commercial capital of the country in the Far East. As usual, after the immigration formalities I proceeded to the baggage section. I identified my baggage and picked them. I needed to go to the gents. "Passengers should not leave their bags unattended." I heard the announcement as I was about to put my bag down and go to the gents. The announcement was repeated several times. While in the gents I was astonished. Right from the entrance I was to be careful with my steps. With my baggage on both hands I walked as if crossing a river on slippery stepping-stones. One mistake and I could find my feet stepping on something relieved on the floor. The standard of the gents made me flash my mind back to my days in *Changanyiko* in the Precious Stone Town. The gents were not any better to the common washrooms in *Changanyiko*. To my amazement I saw someone squatting on a tattered mat. The man was right there in the gents, begging. I saw two different worlds between the seemingly posh gentlemen in the terminal lounge and the beggar in the gents.

Outside the gents someone almost intercepted me. He offered to carry my luggage. I did not resist for I thought that must be the hospitality of the people of the land. I appreciated with a nod of my head and I handed the luggage to him. He led me to the taxi bay.

"Ok thank you," I said when we reached a taxi. I stretched out my hand to take the bag. "Give me baksheesh," he replied in a husky voice. "I thought you were just helping me," I remarked. He held his teeth. "Yes I helped you that is why you have to pay baksheesh." He said harshly.

I yielded. I drew some money from my pocket and stretched my hand. He literally snatched the money from my hand.

CHAPTER 18

PRECIOUS STONES ARE NOT
FOREVER

Towards the end of 1999 I had an opportunity to visit the Precious Stone Town. I was in Shinyanga town and my heart was burning to see once more the place where I attended my primary education and a good part of my childhood took place there.

A friend of mine gave me a ride in his car to the town. The road from Mapozeo to the town was not the one I saw sixteen years earlier. On both sides of the road were heaps of sand, hundreds of them.

Half a century after the first geologist discovered the precious stone; new discoveries had been made all over the place. Spontaneous mining involving men with their picks and spades left no land upturned. I was told that the rush for the precious stones would not spare any place. Even people's homes were not spared for that matter. The small miners did not need the D8s, D6s, the draglines and *Manyunguleti*. Picks and spades that was all that they needed.

We reached the main gate of the mine. After some procedures, not as strict as it used to be we were allowed to go in. After all, seemed a mere formality as the security fence in several places was torn apart.

We passed through the churches, then *Uhindini* and near the School. I showed my friend the classroom I used to sit in as a Standard Seven pupil. In 1972 it was labelled STD VIIC. I also showed him the carpentry workshop of the school and what used to be the fine art classroom. They were no longer so.

We drove along the *Uzunguni* avenues. Many houses had broken glass windows. In some houses I saw the broken parts of the windows covered with iron sheets. The houses no longer radiated the civilization and the power of money they used to radiate in the old days. Walls had bleached. They needed to be painted. Flowers were dying from lack of care. The boys' quarters were dilapidated.

We made a turn at the roundabout near what used to be quarters of the men who protected the precious stones. The men had left and some other protection arrangement was in place. We passed near the hospital, I remembered Dr Weiti, of course, he left many years back to his home country across the Indian Ocean.

From the hospital we drove along the town's main road towards the Exclusive club. We passed the golf course or what used to be a golf course on our left. It had overgrown grass. We stopped at what children used to call *duka la Wazungu*. Those days the shop had all types of sweets, breads, cakes, beef, fruits and vegetables from the garden. Those days you could not miss the aroma of the fresh loaves of bread, cakes and imported apples.

We entered the supermarket. The self-service system had been abandoned. Wooden shelves had replaced glass shelves. The bakery that used to make loaves of bread and cakes had been closed. The aroma from fresh breads and cakes that used to fill the air around the bakery was no more. The section of the supermarket, which used to sell clothes, sold maize and other grains packed in sisal sacks. What a change!

That was enough. We came out of what used to be a supermarket and the parking lot (those days it used to be full of cars of every make). The parking lot of the shop was almost empty. I stood there for a while.

We proceeded with our tour through *Uhindini*. I did not see the guava trees. Not as visible as they used to be those days. I saw the house, which Bapu used to live. I remembered the story of the boy who was ready to be slapped three times in order to receive three guavas. We went through the *Changanyiko* blocks. Some houses looked so dilapidated that I suspected they were no longer inhabitable.

We drove through Tabora road. While on Tabora road, I remembered Mama Masozi, the family friend who took me to Dr Weiti, the dentist, many years back. She lived in one of the houses along that road. We proceeded to *Uhunini*, we passed the community centre, block L and outside the main gate. The *askari* on duty waved a goodbye sign and we waved back. Outside the main gate released the breath I had held throughout the tour.

Outside the gate I came out of the car and stood arms akimbo and wondered what was happening to the loyal workers, who knew nothing but to work for the GPMCL.

I was relieved by the fact that my uncle had long retired working for the company. He retired to farming after serving the company faithfully for over thirty years. I knew him to be a hard working fellow. It was however, saddening that there wasn't much to see in terms of his retirement benefits. It seems that financial turbulence had hit the Company at the time when those who were supposed to take care were too relaxed to notice it approaching.

I was still standing within the main gate area as I struggled with all these issues. Out of desperation, I walked into a telephone booth. I dialed a local number. I could hear the phone ringing on the other end. The receiver was picked and a heavy confident voice roared: "Hi!" It was my old friend Ricardo.

"Hi," I answered.

"I've just visited the town!" I said.

"Oh, so you have been in town. So, why didn't you pop in at my home?" he lamented.

"I am sorry, I just couldn't afford it. Time was not on my side," I apologized.

"It is alright," he responded politely.

"How do you see the future of GPMCL?" I asked.

Ricardo answered in a loud and clear voice "Hanging in the balance."

We hung up. I walked out of the booth.

Chapter 19

Sharing the Message

In one cloudy afternoon in 2003, several drummers arrived at a village weekly market pitch earlier than the singers. They gently beat the drums. Gradually but steadily the audience of men, women and children got captivated by the rhythm. As time went by more and more people arrived at the pitch.

That Saturday was not a market day. The villagers were gathering in order to participate in training on an approach to community development. The approach was called Participatory Evaluation Process. It was in Mwamadilah village in Shinyanga Rural District. I was there not only to learn about the approach but also to assist in the facilitation process.

Then the drummers skillfully changed the beats of the drum to accommodate the singers who had arrived. A band of the singers led by *manju* an active and enthusiastic young man joined the drummers with a song.

The voice of the singers and the drum beats blended well. The audience responded by nodding their heads. Some started singing after the *manju*. The first song was over and the *manju* started another song. The active audience turned into passive and solemn listeners. The band of singers continued with the song:

Ishimba elimila abakwetaga bujingi na bumila.

Ishimba uluyumandima ubangandyanga na kumamila.

Tuleke umumalaya tukushila ishimba ilimilya banho ng'ari.

The song translated into English would read:

The lion swallows those who indulge themselves in adultery and prostitution.

They are caught, thinned and swallowed by the lion.

Let us relinquish adultery and prostitution or else we shall perish.

The man- eating lion is fierce.

Having been absorbed by the drum beat not many people noticed a person who was staggering towards the pitch. He reached the pitch and mingled himself with the audience then came and sat next to me. As the *manju* refrained the verse "Ishimba elimila abakwetaga bujinga na bumila" the person echoed it.

I realized that the person was drunk while he must have sensed that I was a stranger. Basing on this presumption he judged that I could not derive the meaning out of the song. Thus he whispered in my ear "the man-eating lion they are talking about is that modern disease".

Back home in my community, more or less, the same euphemism was applied as a substitute for the term that referred to HIV and AIDS. Thus, I could understand what the person was saying. My people had different words for defining illnesses. The word *isekema* was used to define a light fever. The word *indamwa* was used to define a serious illness that could put someone in bed for several days. And the word *imbungo* was used to define a very serious illness that could even incapacitate the victim for a number of months if not for life.

When the modern and incurable disease emerged none of the above words could be used to define it. But the people had to find a name for the health anomaly. Thus, like the people of Mwamadilah, the people in my home area settled at the name "the modern disease".

One day I was attending a funeral in a village in Rungwe district. I joined a group of mourners. We were expecting pastor Mujegemaso Mwebandu, to lead the burial ceremony. I was aware that the people bestowed a lot of respect on the pastor. Thus despite the cold weather the people looked patient.

When the pastor arrived he was welcomed by elders and led into a room that was arranged for him. After a while the pastor came out of the room in his priestly vestments. He then led the mourners into the liturgy for the burial ceremony in accordance with the tradition of the church. After the liturgy he started to deliver what would be a long pastoral message. He explained that he used to visit the deceased during his illness. He told the solemn audience that he had several counselling sessions with the deceased.

Pastor Mujegemaso Mwebandu did not reveal what the deceased confessed to him before he died. But wisely he linked the death to *imbungoimbalapala*. But as time went by people acquired new experiences in their environment and developed new ways of defining things. This is what happened to the modern disease or *imbungo impalapala*. People formulated a new name for the incurable health anomaly. They called it *kisafeti*. The term was, however, used in very informal situations and from a certain perspective it could be interpreted as impolite.

Kisafeti was a corrupted version of sulphate. It was actually the plastic bag that contained the fertilizer that the farmers applied in their farms. The very plastic bag that carried sulphate, an essential nutrient for increasing crop production, posed potential death to the farmers' cow.

From their experience the farmers discovered that the cow that eats a *kisafeti* would certainly die. Nobody had found a veterinary solution to save the life of a cow that had swallowed a *kisafeti*. After applying the fertilizer farmers had to be careful on how they disposed the *kisafeti*. The complicated part of it was that naturally cows were attracted with the salty taste of the sulphate grains that would always remain in the plastic bag. Once a cow gets hold of the *kisafeti* with her mouth a farmer would have to really struggle to pull it out. The cow would use her rough tongue to pick the bag. And the salty taste would motivate the cow to have more of the material inside her mouth. She would chew the plastic bag in order to get every bit of the salty material. The upper and lower jaws would move rhythmically yet careful enough not to let the *kisafeti* slip out of the mouth. You could tell the extent to which the cow enjoys the taste of the *kisafeti* (with the remains of sulphate grains) by the way it moves her tail. The poor cow would not know that she would be chewing her last.

After minutes of chewing, the *kisafeti* would be inside the cow's mouth. It would then get swallowed. The swallowing process would push the thing down the cow's throat. The thing would get stuck in the cow's intestines. Even the ruminant nature of the animal would not be able to bring the thing back to the mouth to be chewed again.

Unfortunately, the digestion system of a cow simply cannot manage the *kisafeti*. Instead the *kisafeti* would cause the dysfunction of the system. And the cow would fail to eat any more food. It would starve until death.

The pastor reminded the people that they first heard about *imbungo imbalapala* (now *kisafeti*) when it hit overseas countries. He proceeded and said: "When we first heard about this incurable disease, we ridiculed the news. We argued that it would never cross those vast seas. Then we heard that our country's commercial capital had also been hit by the disease. We still ridiculed the news. We argued that after all the location of our district is too remote; how can the disease reach us from that far away coastal city? Then, Mbeje, the nearest major town was also hit. We still cheated ourselves that the anomaly would never hit us here in the middle of the banana *shambas*."

The pastor continued to preach to his solemn audience. "Now my brethren, our community is already hit by the incurable anomaly. Many a people die these days. And people talk in whispers, but impolitely, that so and so died because he swallowed a *kisafeti*."

In what was clearly to be the bottom line of his message the pastor said: "The prevalence of HIV and AIDS is not *akapango* but a reality."

CHAPTER 20

THE HORIZON UNVEILED

On my fiftieth birthday, 24th April 2009, I am happy and thankful to the Creator. Moments of reflection normally come to my mind in the afternoon. When the sun is hot I sit under the shade of a big acacia tree within the compound of my home. Then the good and bad memories would pass through my mind.

The memories date as far back as 1965 when I was six years old. I appreciate the fact that so many changes have taken place since then. I liked as well as disliked some of the changes.

For example, I have disliked the environmental deterioration that was taking place in my home village. I started noticing the changes in 1973, when I went back to the village. I had been away for seven years; for the seven years I attended primary education in the Precious Stone Town.

The situation environmental wise has not improved, especially when I think of the several banana varieties that used to exist during my childhood. Leave alone the wild fruits that used to be my favourite in my childhood. Many of the wild fruits I used to enjoy those days are nowhere to be seen largely because of uncontrolled human "development" activities. Even some streams that used to flow with cool and clean water from the hills beyond our village, have either hardly any water to flow or have dried up. Would somebody somewhere do something?

I also miss the way my home town had different communities in 1965 up to early 1970s. Tukuyu, that hometown of mine, had a considerable population of Indians, some Arabs, Somalis and a distinct Swahili community. I liked that.

I was proud of my hometown. In the evenings the single main street in the hometown was a mosaic of Wanyakyusa-Africans, Indians, Arabs, Somalis and Swahili-Africans. I wished the situation had not changed.

Though I have my permanent address in Dar es Salaam I at least once in a year pay my homage there. Whenever I visit home, I cannot avoid seeing the building of the Last Church, the one that my grandfather helped to build as a leader of the denomination in the area. This has remained a big puzzle for me, what did they really mean by "The Last Church"? If my grandfather and his fellow followers meant that there was no other Christian denomination that would be formed after theirs, then they were absolutely wrong. Today, figures have it that there are over 300 Christian denominations in Mbeya region. It seems as if there is a new church being 'born' after every few weeks.

It is also unfortunate that my second home, the Precious Stone Town, is in a dilapidated state. To me how the town was from 1966 to 1972 was a classic example of well managed townships.

During the span of fifty years I have experienced moments of serious illnesses. But I came to realize that even such difficult moments provided opportunities for learning new things that contributed to my personal development. After coming out of the illnesses I appreciated the resultant changes. For example, my interaction with Rastafari changed my eating habit. Before

I eat something I ask myself a number of questions: What is the nutritious value of the food? Is the food safe? When should I eat it?

The travels that I have had inside and outside the country have enabled me to change my world view from the narrow perspective, impressed by the myth of the horizon, to several and broader perspective. The myth hypnotized my mind during part of my childhood. Now I feel free from the hypnotization; I have unveiled the horizon.

EPILOGUE

"… but as he ran through the Maze, he thought about what he had already learned. Haw now realized that his new beliefs were encouraging new behaviours… He knew that when you change what you believe, you change what you do."

-Spencer, *Who Moved my Cheese*

Printed in the United States
by Baker & Taylor Publisher Services